The Beautiful Machine

Maggie Lettvin

BALLANTINE BOOKS • NEW YORK

Dedicated
To my mother
to whom all things are possible.

Acknowledgments
I am grateful to many people, among them: William J. Gibbs, who knocked me into my life's work; Erna Sporer, the teacher who inspired me to go out on my own; Ruth Nelson, who said, "Come to M.I.T."; and M.I.T., which gave me room and permitted me to pass on my ideas to others; WGBH-TV, which backed me in helping countless others to help themselves; and the WGBH crew, each one of whom always did his best for the show and for me; David Atwood, my director, and Charlotte Michaelson, associate producer; the Knopf staff members who worked hard to produce a really usable exercise book, particularly Tony Schulte, Jane Garrett, Susan Arensberg, Charles Schmalz, and Ellen McNeilly; and Steve Wasserman, whose photographs made me look better in 24 hours of shooting than 8 years of work did. I am, of course, especially grateful to Ellen Neuwald, my agent and trustworthy, scrupulously fair adviser; Jerry, my husband, who has set me an example of constant change, study, and caring; and Rick Hauser, my producer, who from a fantastic personal sensitivity brings out the most essential in everything he touches and makes imaginative variations on them, taking all the immense care for which he is well known.

Photographs by Steve Wasserman.
Furniture courtesy of D/R International, Inc.,
and Knoll International Ltd.
Weights courtesy of Elaine Powers Figure Salon

Library of Congress Catalog Card Number: 73-171121

SBN: 345-24253-X-225

This edition published by arrangement with Alfred A. Knopf, Inc.

First Printing: January, 1975

Printed in the United States of America

BALLANTINE BOOKS
A Division of Random House, Inc.
201 East 50th Street, New York, N.Y. 10022
Simultaneously published by
Ballantine Books, Ltd., Toronto, Canada

Contents

The Exercise Planning Guide

THE
EXERCISE PLANNING GUIDE

INTRODUCTION

About seven years ago Maggie suffered a bad whiplash in an automobile accident. Before the injury, however, she had already been complaining of back and leg pains and uncomfortable joints. Admittedly she had a basis for the complaints—a slipped disc in her lower back and an easily dislocated shoulder. Her joints actually creaked—and still do. However, the whiplash injury was her saving. Having spent that winter in constant pain, unable to move her arms much without crying out, she quite suddenly decided that this was a ridiculous way to spend her life. The turning point came when one doctor suggested that she might need surgery on her neck.

She began to rehabilitate herself in a deliberate way. Rather than restrict her movements, she began to extend them a little at a time with daily practice, moving cautiously at first so as to find out what really hurt and what was only a bit uncomfortable. With anatomy books in hand and with the encouragement of a benignly disposed professor of orthopedics, she recovered in about a year and a half, designing her own exercises on the basis of what she had been told was wrong with her. She not only recovered in that time, she also emerged in better shape than she had been for several years.

This kind of success story is what you occasionally get from the advertisements at the backs of magazines and from inspirational articles in those periodicals that grace the check-out counters of supermarkets. Usually the recovery is tied to a particular method of exercise or a semi-religious discipline. We tend too easily to discount these stories, because they seem to be tied to a kind of magic. But we ought to look at them more closely, for the testimonials are probably not faked. The people probably really did get better for having tried whatever discipline they are praising.

The critical factors—and they are very critical—in all these recoveries as well as Maggie's—are three:

First, there must be a will to improve.

Second, there must be a method or discipline that is followed steadily and actively.

Third, there must be the patience to achieve many successive short-range goals rather than a single, massive, miraculous improvement.

In a striking way, rehabilitation of one's body is very much like learning to play a musical instrument well. There is simply no shortcut to competence in a few days or even a few weeks. But what does happen one week after another is that you can do what was just beyond your ability the week before.

In an age of wonder drugs and overnight cures for some diseases, we tend to confuse recovery with rehabilitation. But a patient can recover well from a heart attack, for instance, and yet remain permanently crippled if he does not slowly and steadily bring himself back as much as he can to normal activity. The same is true for people who have had major surgery, or who have lost a limb, or who even have been paralyzed. However, the most insidious disease of all, that of growing older and less active, does not have a wonder cure. The consequences of a sedentary and restricted life show very quickly at all ages from childhood to the most advanced years. The whole body is maintained in an active way—what is used develops, what is not used diminishes (and that is true for mind as well as muscle). This continuous reorganization, however, is not the basis for despair but of hope. It assures you that, whatever your age, practice always will improve your performance.

Thus, Maggie did not enjoy a miracle; rather, she learned to use and develop her body—something that cannot be done passively, cannot be done *for* you. It is this learning to use which is the basis for all rehabilitation.

In these exercises she does some very sound things regarding the three critical factors mentioned above:

First of all, she exhorts you to want improvement not by suggesting that you will become a Greek god or goddess, but rather that you can become more comfortable with what you have if you can improve what you have. And second, she sets up many subsidiary goals, so that one can measure improvement steadily, even if it is small. That is the essence of good teaching anywhere and reinforces strongly the patience needed to become a virtuoso with one's own equipment.

Not only as Maggie's husband but also as a medical man, I am very impressed by her present fitness. I can testify that, although she tries to hide them publicly, she still suffers the same occasional discomforts, aches, pains, and so forth that everyone else does. But she has learned to bounce back quickly, function with small disorders, and overcome the lassitude and depression that comes on with bodily discomfort. Because she has learned to move freely, she looks better and happier as she gets older.

Best of all, she has set her work up not as a method of curing or a way of bypassing medicine, but as a necessary adjunct to it, wherein everybody learns the pleasure of having the soundest body one can have.

JEROME Y. LETTVIN, M.D.

HOW TO USE THE
EXERCISES AND CHARTS

The charts in this "Guide" are designed to give you the most effective exercises for particular parts of your body and for a variety of special problems. Here's how you proceed.

First read the Precautions (page 6) and take them to heart.

Now look through the exercises. Note that there are instructions and photographs for 60 exercises, with 3 versions of each exercise, making a total of 180 exercises. All exercises are given in three variations: Easy, Medium, and Hard.

Return to the "Guide" and look for the chart dealing with the part of your body that needs work (starting on page 12 every area is covered from toes to neck). Here's a sample chart.

EXERCISE	EASY	MEDIUM	HARD
3	√	√	√
5	√	√	√
37		√	

Begin by looking at all of the Easy exercises checked on the chart (in this case #3 and #5). *Be sure to read the entire exercise:* sometimes there is an easier or harder variation included. Now try the exercises.

If an exercise seems too easy, substitute a Medium or Hard version. Select no more than ten exercises at a time. If you prefer, pick out only one or two exercises and keep at them, building slowly over several days, until you see or feel results.

Other Programs

- Starting on page 36 are six programs to fit your physical condition (and improve it)—ranging from a very easy program for the exhausted or bedridden to a very hard training program for athletes.
- Maintenance Programs begin on page 44 and will help you *stay* in shape.
- Basic and Special Exercises for circulation and respiration, endurance, pregnancy, etc., begin on page 49, and Therapeutic Exercises on page 61.

Whatever Program You Choose Remember This:

1. Read the Precautions and the section on Time and Exercising.

2. You don't have to do all the exercises on any given chart. Do no more than ten different exercises in one session unless you are accustomed to exercising and know your own body well. If you overdo, you'll become tired and discouraged.

3. When you begin a new series, always start with easy versions. Whenever any exercise begins to feel too easy to be productive, substitute an exercise in the next hardest category. Save the easy one for warming up.

4. Don't model your program on someone else's. There is no reason why any two people should exercise at the same time or in the same way unless they choose to do so.

5. Just don't overdo. Any time of day is fine! Any place is fine! Any reason is fine! Any speed is fine!

Quite literally, *moving* keeps the body and soul together. Pull *yourself* together! Exercise!

PRECAUTIONS

A hot bath before exercising helps you to be more flexible.

Wear loose warm clothing for the exercising if possible. Be barefoot if possible. If impossible—exercise anyway. Always start each exercise period, no matter how short, slowly!

Check each exercise for cautions before beginning! And don't do anything that hurts without a doctor's special permission and advice. If you suspect that you have something wrong with you, get checked over by a doctor before beginning. And if you are under a doctor's care for any ailment at all, don't begin before consulting him.

Be sensible. Be cautious. Remember that you must be guided by common sense whether you see a specific caution or not. Start with the easiest of the exercises. Do them slowly and carefully to find which ones you can do without too much trouble and preferably with no discomfort. Don't try exercises that are too difficult for you to do right now.

The first time you try any exercise, no matter how good your condition, *do it gently!* And *always bounce gently—stretching takes time!* Be sure to taper off from each exercise period slowly! Save a few of the easier exercises for warming up and tapering off, especially the easy circulation–respiration exercises.

If you have a headache or fever, *don't exercise!* However, exercising when you have a cold or sinus condition tends to clear the passageways. After any period without exercise, whether because of sickness or not, *begin slowly* again and build up. *Be consistent!* Your body really needs daily exercise, just as it needs daily food and daily rest.

A hot bath after exercising helps to keep you from getting stiff if you've worked too hard.

Unusual possibilities: If you get dizzy, feel faint, or seem to be blacking out, drop down to the floor or a bed immediately. As soon as you feel okay, begin again. Don't work quite as hard. If the feeling continues it's best to see a doctor.

If you bruise yourself, press an icy wet cloth firmly against that part for three minutes to cut down on the bleeding under the skin. Then move the furniture!

If you get a cramp, don't continue to work until you stretch the cramp out and massage or knead it deeply with your fingers or the heel of your hand. Start gently if it really hurts and then dig in more and more until the cramp eases out. If it's a really bad cramp you may still feel it a little, for anywhere from an hour or two to a few days. Hot tubs help a lot!

If you do anything serious, such as dropping a weight on your foot or turning or slipping so that you really injure yourself, see a doctor at least for a diagnosis. If you don't know how much or what kind of damage you've done, you can't help yourself properly.

Also, if for any reason you actually hurt—feel pain, not just stiffness—while exercising or afterwards, see a doctor. Pain is a signal letting you know that something is wrong somewhere.

ABOUT
EXERCISING

The necessities

Circulation is how your body is irrigated by blood. *Respiration* is the ability to get oxygen to your tissues. These are the key necessities.

Flexibility is measured by how much freedom you have to move any joint in any direction.

Your *endurance* is good if you can keep doing a lot of physical work without getting tired.

Your *strength* is better the more easily you can handle your own weight.

After the necessities—The bonuses!

Coordination is measured by how smoothly you can move as you want, how well you can get all your muscles to work together.

Balance is measured by how easily you keep yourself from falling.

Agility is measured by how well you can control rapid changes of direction of movement.

Speed is measured by how fast you can go.

Reaction time is a measure of how quickly you can respond.

Your *power* is better the more rapidly you can increase speed. Whether it is an arm, a leg, or your whole body.

TIME AND
EXERCISING

Time—None

No time at all for exercise? To get in better shape move more quickly at all your normal activities. This makes better use of your muscles—and your time. Wear flat shoes so that your feet can move your body in the best possible way, or do yourself an even greater service —go barefoot! Practice walking with proper posture at all times. That all by itself is an excellent exercise.

While you're doing other things, include simple exercises that don't require much concentration. Choose those exercises that you need most.

Sit in a rocking chair instead of a straight one. And don't stand still; rock on your heels or fidget. It's good for you!

Time—In spurts

If you have short periods of time off and on all day, you can put them to good use even if it's only a minute or two, by choosing a few of the best exercises for you and doing one of them every time you have a free minute. Fifteen two-minute periods could keep you in rather good shape. With the right exercises it could keep you in beautiful shape.

If you're in poor condition choose three or four important ones that are reasonably simple and do them all in your few minutes, not tiring any part of you too much. If your condition is good pull out fifteen tough "All Over's." Do just one for the few minutes you have available. That's a lot of good endurance work.

Time—Fifteen minutes

Just about fifteen minutes for exercise?

If your work keeps you on your feet and moving fast

all the time, use your fifteen minutes for abdominals, trunk flexibility, and any other exercises that you need especially.

If you have a job which keeps you standing still (terrible!), be sure to use a lot of your fifteen minutes for circulation–respiration exercises. There are a few that get both your abdominal muscles and also keep you breathing fast. Those will be the best of the lot for you, unless you're not in good condition yet.

If you're overweight, it's more important to walk during your lunch hour than to eat. If you insist on eating, take it with you and have a picnic while you walk.

Time—Half an hour

Half an hour a day is enough time to have your body making great improvements every day. There's no need to push yourself hard. Slowly and steadily you will rebuild (or maybe build for the first time) the strength you need for work, play, or better health.

It really isn't "youth" we're looking for, it's "well-being." We can have it with the proper use of just one half hour a day. Make sure you choose those exercises that are most important for you personally!

Time—One .hour

With a whole hour a day you can get and stay in top shape and continue to improve steadily and reasonably fast. Always include some exercises for circulation–respiration, some for flexibility, and some for endurance. No matter what kind of condition you're in when you begin to exercise, you can find something in each group that you are capable of doing.

Time—All day

If you're lucky enough to have your whole day free to exercise, even if it's only for a few weeks, you can do better by yourself than if you went to a health spa.

Choose a variety of exercises for those areas you would most like to change, and those you most need. They do not need to be impossibly hard, especially since you've got lots of time. Be sure to keep to a few gentle exercises for the first several days. Start with just enough to make you just reasonably tired. Then rest, preferably with windows open and feet up higher than your heart.

If you're a real beginner it may be a good idea to take your rest periods in a tub of hot water with your feet propped way up. When you feel rested, try a few more exercises. Don't repeat exactly the same few over and over. You want to get a lot of muscles a little stiff, not a few muscles very stiff. Repeat this routine day after day, taking as many hot baths as you need to help you to get over any stiffness more quickly.

Gentle circulation–respiration exercises will also help your body get over being stiff. Walking or even gentle running in place for every other exercise period will help out on unstiffening you. So will massaging the stiff muscles. Dig in gently but deeply. Remember that the stiffening means that you are using that part of you well. But don't let any one part get too stiff!

Take the first day very easy! It takes an unused body a while to realize what's happening to it. Don't get discouraged! Results tend to start showing sort of all at once! Be patient! Most important—be consistent!

PROGRAMS FOR ALL PARTS
OF YOUR BODY

Toes—Flexibility and strengthening

These exercises won't seem silly to you if you have the problem of toes that are no longer flexible. They can really create a lot of other problems. It gets hard to walk, it's hard to buy comfortable shoes, and so forth. Besides, they usually look terrible. Here are some exercises that can help to loosen them up.

EXERCISE	EASY	MEDIUM	HARD
1	√	√	√
2	√	√	√
3	√	√	√

Feet—Flexibility and strengthening

Uncomfortable feet make you want to stop moving. Help them out with these.

EXERCISE	EASY	MEDIUM	HARD
1	√	√	√
3	√	√	√
4	√	√	√
5	√	√	√
6	√	√	√

Feet—Flat

Flat feet ruin all your shoes—and hurt!

EXERCISE	EASY	MEDIUM	HARD
1	√	√	√
3	√	√	√
4	√	√	√

Feet—Poor circulation

Do you have cold feet all the time, sometimes turning a funny color?

EXERCISE	EASY	MEDIUM	HARD
1	√	√	√
3	√	√	√

Feet, ankles, calves—Short tendon

Can you get your knees flat when you sit on the floor, legs outstretched?

EXERCISE	EASY	MEDIUM	HARD
3	√	√	√
5	√	√	√
57		√	

Feet, ankles, calves—Footdrop

You can't get the front of your foot up off the floor? Here's possible help.

EXERCISE	EASY	MEDIUM	HARD
6	√	√	

Knees—Flexibility

There are yards of connective tissue here to protect you and help keep your knees flexible. All you have to do is make use of it. *Gently!*

EXERCISE	EASY	MEDIUM	HARD
8	√		
11	√	√	√
18	√	√	√
19	√	√	√
27	√	√	√
30	√	√	√

Knees—Strengthening

The most miraculous piece of equipment will break down without the proper care. Have small knee problems? Don't wait for them to get worse. Start repairing now!

EXERCISE	EASY	MEDIUM	HARD
8	√	√	√
9	√	√	√
10	√	√	√
11	√	√	√
13	√	√	√
16	√	√	√
18		√	√
29	√	√	√

Thighs—Outer

Saddlebags (big bulges at the point where your hands hang on your thighs)? Weak knees? Widening bottom? Get them all at the same time with these exercises!

EXERCISE	EASY	MEDIUM	HARD
9	√	√	√
10	√	√	√

EXERCISE	EASY	MEDIUM	HARD
13	√	√	√
14	√	√	√
16	√	√	√
17	√	√	√
25	√	√	√
29	√	√	√
36	√	√	√
39		√	√

Thighs—Inner

Inner thighs soft and flabby? If they look as though they're hanging there instead of being round and firm, you've got some rewarding exercises ahead of you.

EXERCISE	EASY	MEDIUM	HARD
9	√	√	√
10	√	√	√
11	√	√	√
13	√	√	√
14	√	√	√
16	√	√	√
18	√	√	√
19	√	√	√
25	√	√	√
35		√	√

Thighs—Front

If you need to use your arms to sit down in a chair— or to get up out of it—you really need to do these. Weak muscles here make you feel very "weak in the knees."

15

EXERCISE	EASY	MEDIUM	HARD
9	√	√	√
10	√	√	√
11	√	√	√
13	√	√	√
14	√	√	√
20	√	√	√
25	√	√	√
29	√	√	√
35	√	√	√
37	√	√	√
38	√	√	√
44			√

Thighs—Back

The backs of your thighs and your bottom usually will give out together, quite often oozing like tapioca, as the law of gravity pulls the soft muscle down. The situation is recoverable!

EXERCISE	EASY	MEDIUM	HARD
7	√	√	√
10	√	√	√
12	√	√	√
14	√	√	√
15	√	√	√
17	√	√	√
35	√	√	√
37	√	√	√
39		√	√

Thighs—Flexibility (of muscle)

To make your thighs flexible, you need to stretch not only the joints but also the muscles and their attachments.

EXERCISE	EASY	MEDIUM	HARD
14	√	√	√
18	√		
19	√	√	√
20		√	√
27	√	√	√
36		√	√

Hips—Flexibility

Only one set of exercises is needed to get the hip joint flexible in almost every possible direction.

EXERCISE	EASY	MEDIUM	HARD
14	√	√	√

Hips—Strengthening

So many of us have our major problems from the waist to the knees. Those movements will get much of this area.

EXERCISE	EASY	MEDIUM	HARD
7	√	√	√
9	√	√	√
10	√	√	√
11	√	√	√
12	√	√	√
13	√	√	√
15	√	√	√

16	√	√	√
17	√	√	√
18		√	√
20	√	√	√
29	√	√	√
36	√	√	√

Bottom—Outside

Bottom getting wider and wider? Choose your antidote below. It'll work. We all sit too much or eat too much or both.

EXERCISE	EASY	MEDIUM	HARD
1	√	√	√
7	√	√	√
9	√	√	√
10	√	√	√
12	√	√	√
13	√	√	√
14	√	√	√
15	√	√	√
16	√	√	√
17	√	√	√
18		√	√
29			√
36	√	√	√
37	√	√	√
38	√	√	√
39		√	√

Bottom—Lower

You can squeeze a sagging bottom into a girdle or wear very loose trousers—or you can make the muscles nice and tight again.

EXERCISE	EASY	MEDIUM	HARD
1	√	√	√
7	√	√	√
9	√	√	√
10	√	√	√
11	√	√	√
12	√	√	√
13	√	√	√
14	√	√	√
15	√	√	√
16	√	√	√
37	√	√	√
38	√	√	√

Bottom—Upper

Thickening here? It doesn't just happen with age! As with all muscles, it happens with lack of use.

EXERCISE	EASY	MEDIUM	HARD
1	√	√	√
7	√	√	√
9	√	√	√
10	√	√	√
13	√	√	√
14	√	√	√
15	√	√	√

17	√	√	√
37	√	√	√
38	√	√	√
39		√	√

Bottom—Inside

Those exercises that improve your inner thigh muscles (the ones that pull your leg back in toward your body) will also, for the most part, improve that part of the large muscle of the bottom which is on the inside of the buttocks.

Abdominals—Total sag

Do you feel as if there's no possible way you'll ever get your belly flat again? As long as you have no hernias —and no paralyzed muscles—and are willing to get your weight down too—there's every chance that you'll begin making real progress with these easier exercises.

EXERCISE	EASY	MEDIUM	HARD
21	√	√	
22	√	√	√
23	√	√	
24		√	
25	√		
26	√	√	
27	√		
28	√	√	

When you can go on to the following ones . . .

Abdominals—Front

These are basic for good posture and healthy backs. The number one abdominal exercises!

EXERCISE	EASY	MEDIUM	HARD
20	√	√	√
21	√	√	√
22	√	√	√
23		√	√
24			√
25	√		√
27	√	√	
28	√	√	√
30	√	√	√
33	√	√	√
34	√	√	√
38	√	√	√
39	√	√	√
46	√	√	√

Abdominals—Side

These exercises are for the girdle of Apollo muscles so that your innards don't get squooshed out to the sides by your strong front abdominals.

EXERCISE	EASY	MEDIUM	HARD
16	√	√	√
24			√
25	√	√	√
32	√	√	√
33	√	√	√
34	√	√	√
39		√	√
52	√	√	√

Abdominals—Lower

For carrying babies, for carrying pot bellies, and for carrying yourself well.

EXERCISE	EASY	MEDIUM	HARD
20	√	√	√
22			√
24			√
25	√	√	√
31	√	√	√
39	√	√	√
44			√

Abdominals—In (for pot bellies)

When all your belly muscles are strong and *still* won't stay flat when you stand, try this set.

EXERCISE	EASY	MEDIUM	HARD
26	√	√	√

Abdominals—Specials for the waistline!

Everybody wants a skinny waistline, and luckily your waistline usually changes faster than any other part of your body.

EXERCISE	EASY	MEDIUM	HARD
16	√	√	√
19		√	√
21	√	√	√
22	√	√	√
23	√	√	√
24			√

	EASY	MEDIUM	HARD
25	√	√	√
26	√	√	√
28	√	√	√
30	√	√	√
32	√	√	√
33	√	√	√
34	√	√	√
38	√	√	√
39	√	√	√
46	√	√	√
52	√	√	√

Abdominals—Flexibility

It's most important to strengthen the abdominals, but making them flexible is necessary too.

EXERCISE	EASY	MEDIUM	HARD
20	√	√	√
26	√	√	√
32	√	√	√
33	√	√	√
34	√	√	√
40	√	√	√
46	√	√	√

Back

Bad lower backs have a special section (see page 66). *If your back is bad be sure to take the exercises to your doctor to get his okay. Your* back problem may be different!

Your abdominal muscles should be reasonably strong before you begin to do these back exercises.

Back—Flexibility

What a great feeling to be able to swing freely from your middle!

EXERCISE	EASY	MEDIUM	HARD
14	√	√	√
28	√	√	√
31	√	√	√
32	√	√	√
33	√	√	√
40	√	√	√
46	√	√	√
51	√	√	√
52	√	√	√

Back—Lower

If your back *isn't* in trouble but just needs strengthening, try these.

EXERCISE	EASY	MEDIUM	HARD
15	√	√	√
22			√
25	√	√	√
31	√	√	√
35	√	√	√
37	√	√	√
39	√	√	√
40	√	√	√
50	√	√	√

Back—Middle

Are you gooshy around the waistline in back? Do you slop over your belt?

24

EXERCISE	EASY	MEDIUM	HARD
31	√	√	√
33	√	√	√
35	√	√	√
37	√	√	√
39	√	√	√
40	√	√	√
50	√	√	√

Back—Upper

Do you have flab across your upper back—especially right behind your armpits?

EXERCISE	EASY	MEDIUM	HARD
32	√	√	√
33		√	√
35	√	√	√
36	√	√	√
37	√	√	√
39	√	√	√
40	√	√	√
46	√	√	√
50	√	√	√
52		√	√
56	√	√	√
57	√	√	√

Back—Strengthening (whole back)

Strengthen your back in sections first, then blend them all together. Whole-body movements feel so good!

EXERCISE	EASY	MEDIUM	HARD
7	√	√	√
12	√	√	√
15	√	√	√
18		√	√
22	√	√	√
25	√	√	√
31	√	√	√
33	√	√	√
34	√	√	√
35	√	√	√
36	√	√	√
37	√	√	√
38	√	√	√
39	√	√	√
40	√	√	√
44			√
50	√	√	√
52	√	√	√

Hands—Flexibility

Your sense of touch is most varied in your hands. Keep them as free and strong as possible.

EXERCISE	EASY	MEDIUM	HARD
41	√		

Hands—Circulation

The movement of your hands and arms *also* helps pump the blood back to your heart.

EXERCISE	EASY	MEDIUM	HARD
41	√	√	√

Hands—Strengthening
None of these exercises should be beyond your grasp.

EXERCISE	EASY	MEDIUM	HARD
38	√	√	√
40			√
41		√	√
42	√	√	√
55	√	√	√
56	√	√	√
57	√	√	√

Wrists—Flexibility
Add to the freedom of your hands by getting your wrists more flexible.

EXERCISE	EASY	MEDIUM	HARD
41	√	√	√
43	√	√	√

Wrists—Strengthening
Strength at all joints is necessary if your entire arm is to be strong.

EXERCISE	EASY	MEDIUM	HARD
40			√
42	√	√	√
43	√	√	√
53			√
55	√	√	√

	EASY	MEDIUM	HARD
56	√	√	√
57	√	√	√

Lower arm—Strengthening

You have to use your hands to get your lower arm or forearm strong.

EXERCISE	EASY	MEDIUM	HARD
38	√	√	√
40		√	
41			√
42	√	√	√
43	√	√	√
53			√
55	√	√	√
56	√	√	√
57	√	√	√

Elbows—Flexibility

More freedom of motion!

EXERCISE	EASY	MEDIUM	HARD
43	√	√	√

Elbows—Strengthening

And more strength! These exercises help prevent tennis elbow and other problems.

EXERCISE	EASY	MEDIUM	HARD
49	√	√	√
55	√	√	√
57	√	√	√

Upper arm—Strengthening

Can you carry your own weight—with your arms? You *should* be able to. Men *and* women! Do the following upper-arm exercises.

Upper arm—Front

For lifting and raising objects in front of you with your elbows bent.

EXERCISE	EASY	MEDIUM	HARD
49	√	√	√
53	√	√	√
54		√	√
55	√	√	√
56	√	√	√
57	√	√	√

Upper arm—Back

For pulling and raising your arms behind you (if you can flap your underarms, you're in real trouble).

EXERCISE	EASY	MEDIUM	HARD
35	√	√	√
44	√	√	√
53	√	√	√
55	√	√	√
56	√	√	√
57	√	√	√

Upper arm—Underside

To pull your arms back toward your spine, forward to your navel, or straight down at your side.

EXERCISE	EASY	MEDIUM	HARD
53	√	√	√
55	√	√	√
56	√	√	√
57	√	√	√

Upper arm—Topside

Put your hand on the top of your shoulder just where your shoulder rolls over into your upper arm. That muscle is for pulling and lifting your arm up to the side, up in front and up in back—from the shoulder.

EXERCISE	EASY	MEDIUM	HARD
45			√
53	√	√	√
55	√	√	√
56	√	√	√
57	√	√	√

Shoulders—Flexibility

Loosening up your shoulder joints allows you to move more freely in all directions.

EXERCISE	EASY	MEDIUM	HARD
27		√	√
31		√	√
45	√	√	√
46	√	√	√
47	√	√	√
48	√	√	√
53	√	√	√
55	√	√	√

Shoulders—Strengthening

These are general strengthening exercises from different angles.

EXERCISE	EASY	MEDIUM	HARD
35	√	√	√
36	√	√	√
38		√	√
39	√	√	√
45			√
48			√
49	√	√	√
53			√
55	√	√	√
56	√	√	√
57	√	√	√

Shoulders—Top

Where? Grab your shoulders right by the side of your neck. Those are the muscles we're after here.

EXERCISE	EASY	MEDIUM	HARD
48	√	√	√
53	√	√	√
55	√	√	√
56	√	√	√
57	√	√	√

Shoulders—Front

Important! This area is often neglected.

EXERCISE	EASY	MEDIUM	HARD
45	√	√	√

	EASY	MEDIUM	HARD
49	√	√	√
53	√	√	√
54		√	√
55	√	√	√
56	√	√	√
57	√	√	√

Shoulders—Back

These are strong muscles—easy to build up.

EXERCISE	EASY	MEDIUM	HARD
52			√
53	√	√	√
55	√	√	√
56	√	√	√
57	√	√	√

Shoulders—Strengthening

From lifting a grandchild to carrying a case of beer, we need strong shoulders.

EXERCISE	EASY	MEDIUM	HARD
48	√	√	√
55	√	√	√
56	√	√	√
57	√	√	√

Shoulders—Round and Dowager's Hump

Do you look as though you're carrying the weight of the world on your shoulders? It takes the development of flexibility and strength to straighten up once you've had this bad habit for some time.

EXERCISE	EASY	MEDIUM	HARD
46	√	√	√
50	√	√	√
55	√	√	√

Chest—Flexibility

There's no use making the muscles in the chest strong if you can't stand up straight. Make them flexible first.

EXERCISE	EASY	MEDIUM	HARD
32		√	√
33		√	√
45	√	√	√
46	√	√	√
51	√	√	√
52	√	√	√

Chest—Strengthening

Now make the chest muscles strong!

EXERCISE	EASY	MEDIUM	HARD
18	√	√	√
38	√	√	√
39	√	√	√
41		√	
42	√	√	√
43		√	√
49	√	√	√
53	√	√	√
54	√	√	√
55	√	√	√

33

56	√	√	√
57	√	√	√

Chest—Special for small or sagging breasts

The muscular covering of the chest can be not only tightened, but also made thicker and stronger and molded to a more desirable shape.

EXERCISE	EASY	MEDIUM	HARD
54	√	√	√

Neck—Flexibility

Having a stiff neck is like wearing blinkers! You can't possibly turn your head or neck around far enough to see very much to the side.

EXERCISE	EASY	MEDIUM	HARD
58	√		
59	√		
60	√		

Neck—Strengthening

Once you have your neck flexible you can go on to make it strong.

EXERCISE	EASY	MEDIUM	HARD
40	√	√	
58		√	√
59		√	√
60		√	√

Neck—Front

Do you have a double chin, meaning the muscle or skin droops directly under the chin?

EXERCISE	EASY	MEDIUM	HARD
22	√	√	√
23	√	√	√
24	√	√	√
25	√	√	√
28	√	√	√
46	√	√	√
51	√	√	√
58		√	√
59	√	√	√

Neck—Sides

Jowls? These mean drooping muscle or skin (wattles) to either side of your chin.

EXERCISE	EASY	MEDIUM	HARD
59	√	√	√
60	√	√	√

Neck—Back

If you haven't got a pain in the neck try these.

Problem necks should be in the hands of a doctor. Look for more information under whiplash and cervical arthritis (page 64).

EXERCISE	EASY	MEDIUM	HARD
50	√	√	√
51	√	√	√
58	√	√	√
59	√	√	√
60	√	√	√

PROGRAMS FOR IMPROVING
YOUR CONDITION

No matter what kind of shape you're in there are exercises that you can find here to improve yourself. If you are bedridden, you can pull out very easy exercises that your doctor is sure to approve of. If you are so athletic that you're ready for the Olympics you will find some here that will be helpful, maybe even hard. There is an endless number of ways in which to improve our bodies.

Take the first step.

Very easy lying-down program
for the bedridden

These exercises are for you if you either cannot get out of bed at all or have extreme difficulty in moving about and balancing while on your feet.

Do just a few, several times a day, and strengthen slowly. Keep a chart! Do a few more of each one—each day—if you can!

EXERCISE	EASY	MEDIUM	HARD
1	√		
21	√		
22	√		
23	√		
24	√		
27	√		
41			√

43	√	√	√
48	√	√	
49	√		
50	√		
53	√		
57	√		

Very easy program for the slow beginner

Are you able to get about but not comfortably or easily? These are especially for you if a normal day is an effort.

EXERCISE	EASY	MEDIUM	HARD
1		√	
3	√		
5	√		
14	√		
21	√	√	
22	√	√	
23	√		
24		√	
25	√		
26	√		
27	√		
28	√		
29	√		
30	√		
32	√		
33	√		
47	√		

49	√		
50	√		
51	√		
52	√		
53	√		
57		√	

Easy program for beginners in not too bad condition

If you're healthy but feel tired, slightly depressed, and really out of shape, start in with these exercises.

EXERCISE	EASY	MEDIUM	HARD
1	√		
3	√		
5	√		
8	√		
9	√		
12	√		
13	√		
14	√		
21		√	
22		√	
23	√	√	
24	√	√	
25	√		
26	√		
27	√	√	
28	√	√	
29	√		
30	√		

32	√	√
33		√
34	√	√
36	√	
41		√
46	√	√
47	√	
49		√
50	√	
51	√	
52	√	
53	√	
55	√	
56	√	
57	√	√

Medium Program—Standard

If you can deal with a normal day but get stiff at weekend or vacation athletics—or don't indulge in them because you know you will get stiff—this is your group of exercises.

EXERCISE	EASY	MEDIUM	HARD
1		√	√
3		√	
5	√	√	
7	√	√	
8	√	√	
9	√	√	
10	√	√	
11	√	√	

12	√	√	
13		√	
14		√	
16	√		
21		√	√
22			√
23		√	√
24			√
25		√	
26		√	√
27		√	√
28			√
29		√	√
30		√	
32		√	√
33		√	√
34		√	
36		√	
41		√	
46		√	√
47		√	
49		√	√
50		√	√
51		√	
52		√	
53	√	√	
55		√	
56	√	√	
57		√	√

Hard Program—Athlete

If you're out daily for some kind of athletic program, at least part of the year, you need a general conditioning program year round!

EXERCISE	EASY	MEDIUM	HARD
1		√	√
3		√	√
5	√	√	√
7		√	
8		√	√
9		√	√
10		√	√
11	√	√	
12		√	√
13		√	√
14			√
16		√	
21			√
23		√	√
25			√
26			√
27			√
29			√
30			√
32			√
34			√
35			√
36			√
37		√	√

		EASY	MEDIUM	HARD
38				√
43				√
45				√
47			√	
50				√
52				√
53				√
55				√
56				√

Very Hard Program—Training

If you're in great shape and out for all you can get from your body in every possible direction, every day, play with these.

EXERCISE	EASY	MEDIUM	HARD
1			√
3		√	√
5	√	√	√
7		√	√
8		√	√
9	√	√	√
10			√
11	√	√	√
12		√	√
13		√	√
14	√	√	√
16		√	√
19	√	√	√
22			√

23			√
25			√
26			√
27			√
29			√
30			√
34		√	√
35		√	√
36		√	√
37		√	√
38		√	√
42		√	√
43	√	√	√
44			√
45		√	√
46	√	√	√
47	√	√	√
48		√	√
49		√	√
50		√	√
53		√	√
55		√	√
56		√	√

MAINTENANCE PROGRAMS

Easy program
 To remain capable of handling a day at a time.

EXERCISE	EASY	MEDIUM	HARD
1	√		
5	√		
9	√		
12	√		
13	√		
14	√		
17	√		
25	√		
26	√		
28	√		
29	√		
30	√		
32	√		
34	√		
35	√		
36	√		
37	√		
44	√		
47	√	√	
52	√		

55	√		
56	√		
57		√	√

Medium program
To bubble along happily day after day.

EXERCISE	EASY	MEDIUM	HARD
1		√	
5		√	
7		√	
9		√	
12		√	
13		√	
14		√	
17		√	
25		√	
26		√	√
29		√	√
30		√	
34		√	
35		√	
36		√	
37		√	
47		√	
55		√	
56		√	

Hard program
For an all-around top-notch body prepared to handle quickly and efficiently any problem that happens along.

EXERCISE	EASY	MEDIUM	HARD
1			√
5			√
7		√	
9			√
10			√
12			√
13			√
14			√
17			√
23			√
25			√
26			√
29			√
30			√
34			√
35			√
36			√
37			√
38			√
44			√
47			√
55			√
56			√
59			√

All-over time savers

Everybody wants to be in the best shape possible with the least amount of time spent to get that way. The fastest way to get into—and stay in—good condition is to do exercises that use your whole body at one time. If you can add to that enough movement to also take care of your circulation and respiration you're really moving in the fastest possible way toward "total fitness." Get your whole body turned on—your whole body "thinking"!

If you're new to exercising or not yet in very good condition, be sure to start with "part" exercises first so as not to injure yourself. When you are in pretty good shape "all-over," try doing these as a maintenance program. Be sure to do it safely! *Always begin and end each exercise period slowly!*

Begin with the exercises that use just your arms or your legs actively, and when you feel sure of yourself go on to those that have you moving both ends at once.

EXERCISE	EASY	MEDIUM	HARD
1	√	√	√
4			√
7		√	√
9		√	√
11			√
12	√	√	√
13	√	√	√
15			√
16	√	√	√
17	√	√	√
18	√	√	√
23	√	√	√
25	√	√	√
33			√
35	√	√	√
36	√	√	√

37	√	√	√
38	√	√	√
39	√	√	√
40		√	√
44			√
49		√	√
51		√	√
56	√	√	√
57	√	√	√

BASIC AND SPECIAL EXERCISES

Circulation—Respiration

Circulation is the way your body is irrigated by blood. Respiration is the ability to get oxygen to your tissues.

Unless you can breathe easily and comfortably no matter what your level of activity, you know yourself that you're only half alive. It is extremely important, no matter what your way of life requires of you in the way of movement, to have all your breathing equipment in the best possible working order. Either your entire body is in the best possible condition to use the available oxygen, no matter how little there is, or you're dead! Sometimes it feels as though it's a losing battle trying to deal with the pollution from industry and cars, but a battle we can fight and most often win is with our own pollution processing plant—our bodies!

Yogis call breath "the great bird of life." Beautiful? I also like to think of it as "the great red river." When your blood picks up the oxygen it needs from your lungs, the oxygen makes it appear red. Like a river, your blood deposits some things along its edges as it picks other things up and carries them along. As it deposits its oxygen out along the edges the "river" becomes bluer and bluer. If you train your river to pick up more oxygen and to move faster so that it irrigates more of your local terrain you're bound to have more lush growth in the surrounding areas.

EXERCISE	EASY	MEDIUM	HARD
1	√	√	√

3			√
4		√	√
5		√	√
6		√	√
7			√
9	√	√	√
10		√	√
11	√	√	√
12	√	√	√
13	√	√	√
16			√
18			√
23			√
32			√
33			√
34			√
35			√
38			√
51			√
56			√

Flexibility

Flexibility is measured by how much freedom you have to move any joint in any direction.

You can be as muscular as you want, but if you're not flexible also you're not in the best possible condition! We all need to be flexible, but for athletes it becomes even more important. With the terrific stresses and strains they put on their bodies if their joints aren't free to move, they are likely to end up with injuries that will keep them from enjoying the rest of their lives.

EXERCISE	EASY	MEDIUM	HARD
1	√	√	
3	√	√	√
4	√		
5	√	√	√
8	√		
14	√	√	√
18	√		
19	√	√	√
27	√	√	√
31	√	√	√
32	√	√	√
33	√	√	√
34	√	√	√
40	√		
41	√	√	√
45	√	√	√
46	√	√	
47	√	√	√
48	√	√	
51	√	√	√
52	√	√	
53	√	√	
58	√		
59	√		
60	√		

Endurance

Your endurance is good if you can do a lot of physical work without getting tired. But you have to start somewhere!

There was a time when I couldn't run in place for more than a minute. Today I can run for three hours!

There was a time when I couldn't get my feet up in the air at the same time as my hands while sitting on my bottom. Today I can hold that position for five minutes!

There was a time when I would fall to the floor just trying to get *down* out of a pushup. I could *never* at that time have lifted myself back up. Today I can do five whole, real pushups!

There was a time when I could just barely let myself down out of a chinup slowly. Today I can climb along an overhead ladder several times.

Tomorrow the Olympics—you never know until you try! It really doesn't take *hard* work to build up endurance. You only need to be consistent for it to happen!

These are some of my favorites for endurance, which take in a lot of areas that, for most people, could stand some improvement.

EXERCISE	EASY	MEDIUM	HARD
1	√	√	√
25	√	√	√
33	√	√	√
55	√	√	√
57	√	√	√

Posture

Posture is the way you hold your body while moving or while still. Some postures will injure and weaken your body; some will safeguard and build it. But posture should never be thought of in terms of an unmoving body! If you just stand still and sit still, your body's machinery slows down to the point that all it can do efficiently is stand and sit. Any extra effort will be work instead of a pleasure. Your bones will get fragile, your circulation will slow down, your muscles will lose their strength (including your heart, which is also a muscle). Every part of you will slow down in its ability to do anything other than sit or stand.

Just moving with good posture is exercising your muscles well. Your whole body gets better or worse according to how you move and how much you move. For everyone good posture is a little different. But you should be able to move your own body freely and without pain and without tiring too quickly, in such a way as to maintain yourself in comfortable working order no matter what movements you need to make.

Feet

EXERCISE	EASY	MEDIUM	HARD
1	√	√	√
4	√	√	√

Bottom

EXERCISE	EASY	MEDIUM	HARD
31	√	√	√

Abdominals

EXERCISE	EASY	MEDIUM	HARD
21	√	√	√
22	√	√	√
23	√	√	√
24			√
25	√	√	√
26	√	√	√

EXERCISE	EASY	MEDIUM	HARD
27	√		
28	√	√	√
33	√	√	√
39	√	√	√ .
46	√	√	√

Shoulders

EXERCISE	EASY	MEDIUM	HARD
46	√	√	√

Back

EXERCISE	EASY	MEDIUM	HARD
31	√	√	√
37	√	√	√
39	√	√	√
50	√	√	√

Desk Workers, Commuters, Chair Sitters in General

Look through all the chair exercises to find which ones are best for your problems. Do at odd moments.

EXERCISE	EASY	MEDIUM	HARD
1	√		
2	√	√	
4	√		
8	√	√	
12	√		
16	√		

21	√		
26		√	
28	√	√	
29	√		
30	√		
34	√		
44	√		
45	√	√	
48	√	√	√
49	√		
51	√		
52	√		
53	√	√	√
57	√		
58	√	√	
59	√	√	√
60	√	√	

Pregnancy and Delivery

Pregnancy and delivery require a strong and healthy body if they are going to be as comfortable as they can possibly be. The healthier you are, the healthier your baby will be. You can actually feel great, be comfortable, and look your best all through your pregnancy and—what's more important—afterward!

The aches, pains, discomforts, and clumsiness that are considered usual during pregnancy are almost totally unnecessary. Giving your body just a half hour to an hour's care each day can prevent almost all of these problems. No hard work! Just a slow, steady strengthening of the necessary muscles, circulation, and respiration, and training of the important sphincters.

Exercise may begin any time during your pregnancy. You must, however, begin slowly. Never push yourself hard. Curb your enthusiasm! You can do an enormous amount of good if you are careful. Listen carefully to your body; when it needs rest—rest it! If you are in really sad shape, you can make your exercise periods just a minute long several times a day for the first week or so. Starting as late as the sixth or seventh month you can get into really good shape by the time your delivery date comes around! Even in the ninth month the very easy exercises can do you good! Don't waste any time at all that is available to you. In any case, your doctor should know if you decide to exercise, particularly if you have any physical problems at the time of your pregnancy.

If you haven't been exercising at all before, start with exercises from each group that are practically no effort at all. Do them slowly and steadily, just a few of each in the beginning, and space them out over the day so as not to tire yourself. Build up slowly day by day. You will really have a big surprise to look forward to after delivery. You actually can have a better figure after having a baby than before if you prepare properly.

It is really best, of course, to prepare your body for pregnancy with exercise. If you are smart enough to start ahead of time you can not only work at a faster rate of speed, but you will also be able to do that one set of exercises (see below) that will be impossible to do after about the second month—or about the time you find out that you are pregnant.

EXERCISE	EASY	MEDIUM	HARD
26	√	√	√

If you want to prevent backaches, it is extremely important to wear flat shoes. This along with posture exercises will not only help your back but will also help to prevent stretch marks. If your pelvis is in a position to tip up in front, the weight of the baby on your belly muscles will be less. Wearing high heels will tend to tip the pelvis *back*, which will throw your whole body into the wrong lines. High heels will also throw your balance off, making you feel clumsy.

Walk as much as you can or, if it's impossible to get out, try these exercises.

EXERCISE	EASY	MEDIUM	HARD
1	√	√	

The weight of the baby as he or she grows, hanging out on the belly muscles, will in any case stretch the skin to some extent. It is important to keep the abdominal muscles strong, like a retaining wall, to keep the stretching of the skin to a minimum and to help your back to remain strong. The side and front abdominals work together very efficiently—*if* they are strong! Don't neglect either area.

You'll need lots of all of these exercises, *but be sure to work up very slowly.*

Front abdominals

EXERCISE	EASY	MEDIUM	HARD
21	√	√	√
22	√	√	√
23	√	√	√
28	√	√	√
30	√	√	√

Side abdominals

EXERCISE	EASY	MEDIUM	HARD
25	√	√	
32	√	√	

Posture

All of the exercises for the abdominals and walking will help your posture, but you need a way of checking, judging, and improving your posture aside from them.

EXERCISE	EASY	MEDIUM	HARD
31	√	√	√

Back

As the weight of the baby increases, your back will need to become stronger to hold your pelvis in position. These muscles made stronger will also be very useful after delivery for carrying the baby in yet other positions.

EXERCISE	EASY	MEDIUM	HARD
37	√	√	

Chest flexibility and raising

Making the chest muscles strong will help them to hold up the increased weight of your breasts. If the muscles are not only strong but also flexible, they will really help later on in your pregnancy when you want to lift your chest up to allow yourself more freedom to breathe.

EXERCISE	EASY	MEDIUM	HARD
46	√	√	

Chest building

EXERCISE	EASY	MEDIUM	HARD
54	√	√	

Getting to the floor

You really should be able to sit on the floor now, not

only to keep your hips in good condition but also to get you to the floor easily for your inner-thigh stretching exercises and to prepare you for a few years of lifting your baby up from the floor.

EXERCISE	EASY	MEDIUM	HARD
10	√		

Splits

Split practice loosens up the inner thigh area to prepare you for delivery.

EXERCISE	EASY	MEDIUM	HARD
19	√	√	√

Always end each exercise period with more walking or more of the running in place exercise.

One of the most important exercises for you to do during this period is the training of your lower sphincters. Every time you go to the toilet to relieve yourself be sure that you use a strong stop–start action. The way you do this is first to allow yourself to start going naturally and then, pulling everything up tight, stop the flow hard! Repeat this action over and over again until you can not only do it easily, but can also hold it tight for several minutes at a time if necessary.

The relaxing part of it is going to help you to relax this sphincter on command at delivery, making your delivery much easier for you. This is very important! If, when your uterus is contracting to push the baby out, the sphincters are tightening to hold the baby in, out of a lack of knowledge, you are going to be very uncomfortable.

The tightening-up part of the exercise is to prevent you from wetting yourself when you cough, sneeze, or laugh, now and after the baby is born. It will also give you back your bladder control as quickly as possible after the baby in born.

Postnatal

Immediately after delivery you can begin doing the easiest exercises again. The muscles have been made stronger by their hard work during delivery, but as after any hard work they are also very tired! Strengthen slowly. Start walking as soon as your doctor will allow it (usually immediately)! In just a few short weeks you will see the rest of the fruits of your labors—your body with flat belly, tight waistline, a strong back for dealing with your new baby, and plenty of energy!

EXERCISE AS THERAPY

Varicose Veins

Varicose veins can develop because of too little leg activity, weak connective tissue, or both. The veins begin to expand and turn because of extra pressure they have to handle. They then become longer, and fold on themselves. Luckily this problem almost always starts where you can see it and also, luckily, there are things you can do to slow down what is happening or maybe even to bring it to a complete halt. The sooner you attack it the better! Let any piece of machinery go too far and it gets more and more difficult to repair, with one problem *always* leading to another.

For a more complete explanation, read on if you like. If not, just skip over the next page or so and go on to what you can do to help yourself.

The blood system is called a circulation because the blood that is pumped *out* of the heart *returns* to the heart! The blood goes from the heart through the arteries to a network of small tubes called capillaries, and from the capillaries into veins, and from veins back into the heart. The blood stays enclosed everywhere! Only in the capillaries do food and oxygen pass out of the blood to the body tissues and waste pass into the blood from those tissues.

Arteries are thick-walled, muscular tubes and can stand much pressure. Veins are thin-walled and have no muscle in them! They're only elastic tubes! Along the veins are thin flap-like valves, like doors that open only in one direction, which let the blood flow toward the heart but stop it from flowing back.

Now about *varicose* veins! Varicose means "unnaturally swollen or dilated." There are really two sets of

61

veins: *one set lies just under the skin, and the other lies between the muscles!* The two sets are connected to each other by many short veins. Imagine the veins in your legs, one set under the skin, another set between the muscles, connected° to each other in a one-way ladder arrangement: the blood can only go up in them if they're healthy; it can't go down!

Veins aren't muscular, so if you don't move you have *only* the pressure of the blood coming out of the capillaries to drive this column of blood up to the heart! If you have the kind of job where you stand or sit still for long periods of time, *all the veins fill up with blood!* (The valves, or little flap doors, will stop the blood from flowing back, but as you stand still or sit still the pressure of the column of blood all the way up to the heart presses back down and blows up the veins with blood to the fullest they can get.)

It's about three and a half to four feet from your ankles up to your heart! That's a lot of pressure on those little elastic tubes! The veins between the muscles are supported by the muscles, so they don't blow up as much. But the veins under the skin are much more loosely held, so that sooner or later, with a lot of quiet sitting or standing, the walls of the surface veins begin spreading. This spreading stretches the walls apart near the valves, creating pockets that fill with blood. Their pressure pulls the valves apart even when "closed." So a little gap appears where the blood can flow back!

Then, as if things aren't bad enough, the blood moving slowly in the veins allows bacteria to gather in the little pockets at the sides of the valves (the hinges of the door), and inflammation sets in. Because of the inflammation, scarring sets in (the door hinges get rusty). After a while, not only can the doors, or valves, not prevent the blood from flowing backwards, but even the forward flow is slowed up because of the scarring. With the slowing of the flow the veins become even more inflamed. So they get steadily worse.

Now let's see what happens when you exercise, when you move—walking, running, even just shifting your weight. The muscles of your legs tighten and relax, acting like a pump to squeeze the blood upward from the deep veins. During the time that the muscles are relaxing, not only do the deep veins fill from the flow of blood from the capillaries (remember the valves in healthy legs keep the pumped blood from flowing back down), but also the veins under the skin empty into the deep veins through the cross veins. This is the important part! Since the valves in the veins under the skin prevent the blood from flowing back down, the pressure drops in the section of vein between the valves, *as long as you keep pumping!* This makes the pressure in the veins under the skin on your legs drop from three or four feet of pressure to anywhere from a few inches to about a foot of pressure, depending on how actively you move your legs!

No matter how bad your varicose veins are, there is always something you can do to help yourself!

Sleep with your heels a little higher than your heart.

Whether your legs ache and your ankles swell or not, if you've got varicose veins, rest several times a day with your heels up higher than your heart, for fifteen minutes or so at a time.

While lying down, with your feet higher than your heart preferably, pull the front of first one foot up and then the other, or twist your ankle around. You can also do this sitting in a chair.

While lying down in bed, walk with your feet against a pillow that you have put against the foot of your bed.

Rock in a rocking chair (in a regular chair if you don't have a rocking chair—but rock!).

Walk in place, holding on to the back of a chair if you need to for balance.

Walk. Use a cane if you need to, either for balance or to protect yourself.

Walk up and down stairs.

Walk and jog. Walk first to warm up, jog just a little, walk a little more. Keep it up, starting with a little exercise and doing just a little bit more each day. Always slow down each jogging session by walking for a while.

Try jumping rope. Start slowly; end slowly.

Walk to warm up, then jog-run-jog-walk.

One important point says it all—*keep your legs and feet moving!*

Whiplash, Cervical Arthritis, Painful Neck Conditions

EXTREME CAUTION!! FOLLOW ONLY WITH YOUR DOCTOR'S COMPLETE APPROVAL!!

First some hints: Wearing wool turtleneck shirts or even dickies, twenty-four hours a day, sleeping or waking, will help ease your discomfort some. Choose times other than rush hours to be on the streets: there's less traffic and thus less likelihood of being jostled. Cross in the center of the block to avoid having to turn your head to look for traffic, and when you do have to turn, move from the waist. Watch out for curbs or anything else that might jolt your spine. Wear flat-heeled shoes. Let someone else carry groceries, laundry, children, etc. Let someone else take the dog for a walk. Move your arms slow and carefully—not stiffly—and relax. Avoid kicking anything. Your whole body works together! It'll hurt! Get out of the habit of answering questions with a shake of your head.

Other things to help: Good posture will help your neck recover faster. Use this time to build good habits for the rest of your life. Hold your shoulders slightly down, back of head stretched slightly up. Keep your chin level. *Sometimes* a sling to carry an aching arm helps. Stay aware of your neck! If the pressure of the sling is enough to cause more discomfort, *don't use it!* *Sometimes* a belt, that you can hook the thumb of the aching arm in, helps.

When you ache from your neck condition, take a hot bath. While you're in the water, ease your shoulders down and the back of your head and your neck gently up. Try a towel behind your head to keep your neck from having to work holding your head in this position. Keep your neck under the water. Now (don't laugh; it'll hurt), talk to your muscles! Consciously try to relax them!

If you can't for any reason get into a tub, get into bed this way: Sit on the bed. Let down onto the bed that elbow on the side having the least pain, and then let the rest of your body down without stopping. Lie with a hot, wet towel at the back of your neck with Saran Wrap around it to both protect the bed and keep the heat in. Again, ease your shoulders down and the back of your head up. Put a small folded towel up under the back of your head.

Is there a comfortable position in which you can rest and maybe even sleep? Sometimes pillows or folded towels, placed just right, can allow you to be comfortable.

If you lie on your back, try a pillow or a folded towel right up under the back of your head, shoulders eased down, back of head eased up, and another tucked under the edge of whichever shoulder aches. Sometimes other pillows, to hold your elbow and arm up, can make all the difference.

If you sleep on your side, be sure you use a high, soft pillow above your shoulder, under your head, to keep the weight of your head from pulling your neck at an angle. Another pillow or pillows in front of you to rest your arm on will keep the weight of your arm from pulling on your shoulder and neck muscles.

For a change you could try lying face down with a pillow lengthwise under the top of your chest. Your shoulders and head should roll gently over the edges of the pillow, shoulders to the side, head over forward. This position is not so comfortable. It is hard to get your arms into a position that puts your shoulder muscles at ease. Try them down at your sides. If it's not comfortable, forget it! *Roll* back over! Don't, whatever you do, raise up on your elbows!

When your doctor says you can slowly start exercising, please do any movements for the first few weeks or months only while in "over the door" traction. And only with your shoulders eased down and the back of your head eased up! And only after soaking or using a hot wet towel! Keep your neck warm!

Keeping your whole neck stretched up and your shoulders stretched down the whole time, ease one side of your neck up gently even a little further. Then the other side. Gently pull your shoulders down even a little further from side to side.

Next, with shoulders still stretched down and neck still stretched up, turn your chin gently to the left. *If it hurts, don't go any further!* Stop each time before you get to the point where it hurts! Again, do the same thing to the other side.

Shoulders still stretched down and back of head still stretched up? Staying in traction, relax a little, and then stretch your shoulders and head out in opposite directions again and again, *but gently!*

Keep these exercises up until you can move without pain before going on to any other neck exercises, and then approach them with extreme caution.

Always release the traction very slowly and gently. Five minutes to release slowly may save you hours of discomfort.

Bad Backs

Please use this information only if your doctor agrees, and ask for his help in deciding which exercises to do.

If any of the exercises cause you pain, do not continue without consulting your doctor. Don't just tell him about them! Take this book with you and go to him! Let him help you to choose the right exercises for *you* according to *your condition!*

How to Sleep

Except in a few cases (specified by your doctor), most bad backs feel best when you lie in a knee–chest position with your knees pulled up just far enough for comfort. This stretches out muscles in spasm and relieves the pressure on the joints between the vertebrae.

A pillow between your knees will keep your uppermost leg from dragging on your back. Another pillow by your chest to rest your uppermost arm on can help too. Lie on whichever side feels least uncomfortable, but if the pain is pretty bad, you may find it easiest to sleep with your knees under you and your behind stuck up in the air. Try a pillow across your knees in this position. Or try sleeping on your back, a pillow *under your knees.* In this position, try two more pillows, at either side of your hips, to help prevent strain on unsupported muscles. Keep yourself as warm as possible. If any part of you gets cold, all of your muscles tighten up sympathetically.

How to Get Out of Bed

First, do Exercises 21 Easy, 22 Easy, and 23 Easy to loosen you up a bit. Have your bed arranged so that you can roll over onto the side that bothers you most. Get your legs, from the knee down, over the side of the bed. Push yourself up with your arms so that you are sitting on the bed with your feet on the floor. Move your bottom forward on the bed until you are sitting on the edge with your feet back a little way under you. With your hands on your knees, lean forward, keeping your weight forward until you can lift your bottom off the bed. From this crouch, you can walk your hands partway up your thighs to less of a crouch. Then, using a bureau or a windowsill or anything else that's solid, you can push yourself up with your hands to a standing position.

How to Take a Bath

Get someone to run the tub full of very warm water. Most bathtub faucets are too low for people with bad backs.

Make sure there's a non-skid rubber mat in the tub— and another on the floor outside the tub!

Once you get in the warm tub and relax, do not lie still the whole time. If you move while your muscles relax from the heat, you will be able to move more easily after you leave the tub. Do Exercises 24 Easy and Medium, for example, or just walk your feet against the edge of the tub, keeping both feet on the tub the whole time.

When you get out of the tub, try to have someone with you. Safety before modesty. Don't take chances. Just before you get out, move in as many ways as you can with the least discomfort. You now have some flexibility. Turn on your side and grab the edge of the tub with your upper hand; using the other arm to push, roll over onto your knees and get up. Keep tight hold of the tub while you step over the edge of it and then put your hands on your bent knees and walk them up your thighs until you can shift your hands to a sink or windowsill to help you stand again. Dry yourself and get back into warm clothes as quickly as possible. When you can do more than just move a little in the tub, exercise after your bath; it's the best time. In bed, if it's the best you can do, walk your feet on a pillow propped against the foot of the bed. Another pillow or folded towel can go under your knees for comfort and you can tuck your hands under the edge of your hips.

Walking exercises in any position help improve your circulation. If you don't keep moving your limbs and putting stress on them, calcium will slowly be taken away from the bones. Ask your doctor; maybe you can rock in a rocking chair or even walk.

When you are physically able, begin the exercises for back flexibility and the strengthening of the straight abdominals (the ones that run from your ribs at the top to your pubic bone below). Both the back and the abdominal muscles help your shoulders and hips to pull toward each other. You will build your abdominal muscles from the top and the bottom and gain flexibility in your back with all these exercises.

EXERCISE	EASY	MEDIUM	HARD
1	√		
21	√		

22	√	√	√
24	√	√	
27	√		
28	√	√	
30	√	√	
31	√	√	

Careful, consistent exercise most likely is going to make your bad back better and better. Several times a day is best in the beginning, using just a few of the easiest exercises. As your back improves you can work your way to doing more of the harder ones, only once a day. Be consistent! It'll pay off!

"Instant" Relief

If you have a back that suddenly "goes out," one of the most useful things you can do is stretch your back out within a few minutes after the trouble begins. If you stretch it out before the spasms and irritations take over, you often can get almost miraculous relief. What I use is a strong bar that can be expanded to clamp hard in a doorway. It is clamped so hard that you can safely chin yourself on it (if you could) and it is high enough that you don't bump your head on it. When your back "goes out," get one hand and then the other up to the bar, grab hold of it tightly, and lower yourself gently by bending your knees until your feet are carrying almost no weight. You can't hold long in this position, so stand up again after about half a minute. Do this several times over the course of a few minutes, by stretching first one hip down a little and then the other. Often, especially if you get to the bar soon enough, you can be completely relieved. My husband taught me this trick. Don't try it until you have your doctor's permission and approval.

Breathing Problems

A breathing problem can be one of the most terrifying afflictions. Quite often it catches you so off-guard and so suddenly that you can become frantic with the fear that help will not reach you in time.

More and more, doctors are working with exercises to give some relief to patients. Certainly when the whole body works with greater efficiency, most physical problems become improved, and sometimes disappear completely.

Too frequently people who have breathing problems are so afraid of overexerting themselves and thereby starting an attack that they slowly weaken their bodies more and more by keeping as physically inactive as they can. But if you exercise properly and stay very aware of not overexerting or exhausting yourself, you can begin today to build your whole body into better condition, especially those muscles that help you to breathe more easily. Your major goal should be to lead a more active life in general, moving into it slowly. You should also learn as many ways of using your breathing apparatus as possible. Whistling is especially good. Singing and shouting are also, and none of these need even the smallest piece of equipment. Or you could: blow bubbles, blow up balloons, learn to play water-filled bottles, learn to play a wind instrument.

Here are some good small exercises to practice several times a day.

Inhale as deeply as possible. Make a "kh" sound and as slowly as possible let the air out in a thin stream until your abdominal muscles have to tighten up and the air is all gone.

Purse your lips as if you're whistling, and blow all the air out in as thin a stream as possible until your belly muscles tighten to push out the last bit of air.

Cough the air out in little coughs until your belly muscles tighten and the air is all gone.

If you can, start yourself laughing and laugh until all the air is gone.

At first, before you get into good shape, you'll find that you run out of breath before your belly tightens. With time and practice and some abdominal exercises, you will get better and better at these.

If you know that you have a tendency toward breathing problems, even if you recover seemingly completely, go on with the exercises or some sport that will keep the important parts in working order. Don't take chances! *Ask for your doctor's help and advice with these. He wants you well—but safely!*

EXERCISE	EASY	MEDIUM	HARD
1	√		
21	√	√	√
22	√	√	√
23	√	√	√
26	√		
27	√		
28	√	√	√
30	√	√	√
45	√	√	√
46	√	√	√
47	√	√	√
48	√	√	√
51	√		
52	√	√	√

Be sure to get your doctor to help you choose the right exercises and to advise you! Don't push yourself too hard! Take lots of time. You'll get there!

Frozen, Stiff, or Painful Joints

Frozen, stiff, or painful joints, whatever the cause, must be helped gently to regain their flexibility or you will certainly end up the loser.

Should you work in spite of the pain? Your doctor should help you judge, especially if the problem is fairly new. If the joints are going to hurt no matter how much or how little you move them, why deny yourself full movement? Even small movements will increase local circulation, which can only help matters. Also remember that calcium deposits at the point of injury or the problem area. You need calcium—but not there! If you keep the joint active, you can keep the calcium from building up so that it cuts down movement or causes you pain. If you already have these excess deposits, it is most often to your advantage to put up with some discomfort while you remold or "sculpt" the joint back to full movement. If the joint is very painful even when making very small movements, try the same movement under very warm water, soaking the joint first for fifteen minutes or more, keeping the water as warm as possible!

Do very few exercises, very slowly and very gently for as long as necessary. Move the joint only a tiny bit more each time you feel you can. Stick with the same easy exercise for long periods of time, but increase the amount of movement. Having the joint underwater takes the weight off it. Having the water warm increases the circulation.

Unless the joint can hang freely under the water it's going to be difficult to swing it freely without putting muscle behind it. For the shoulder and the hip joints it will be difficult to do these underwater unless you have a heated pool or a deep tub available. At least soak for a while first to get the benefit of the heat or use hot, wet packs for a while before exercising. Keep putting fresh hot packs on the joint while you exercise.

Make only very slow, gentle movements to begin

with or you'll end up worse than when you started. Expect some discomfort in the beginning, but be patient and consistent with your poor body. It's doing its best.

Always keep the problem area warm, even if it means wearing gloves, scarves, socks, or whatever in the summer. Don't wear anything tight, because it can cut off circulation. Gentle massage of the surrounding area can also relieve a lot of the discomfort.

When you sleep, keep the affected area covered warmly. It helps a lot! It helps even more if you keep your whole body covered warmly whether asleep or awake, at all times!

Elastic bandages are much like girdles. If you need them for the moment, listen to your doctor, but as soon as you're able, *get the area built up!*

Joint problems can occur for many reasons. Show the proper exercise for your problem area to your doctor for advice and suggestions!

Toes

EXERCISE	EASY	MEDIUM	HARD
2	√		

Feet

EXERCISE	EASY	MEDIUM	HARD
1	√		

Knees

EXERCISE	EASY	MEDIUM	HARD
8	√		

Hips

EXERCISE	EASY	MEDIUM	HARD
14	√		

Back—Lower

EXERCISE	EASY	MEDIUM	HARD
22	√	√	√
24	√	√	

Back—Upper (dowager's hump, round shoulders)

EXERCISE	EASY	MEDIUM	HARD
46		√	

Hands

EXERCISE	EASY	MEDIUM	HARD
41	√	√	√

Wrists

EXERCISE	EASY	MEDIUM	HARD
41	√	√	√
43	√		

Elbows

EXERCISE	EASY	MEDIUM	HARD
43	√		

Shoulders

EXERCISE	EASY	MEDIUM	HARD
47	√		

Chest

EXERCISE	EASY	MEDIUM	HARD
47	√		

Neck

EXERCISE	EASY	MEDIUM	HARD
48	√		
58	√		
59	√		
60	√		

Muscular Disorders (weakening and wasting)

These exercises are to be done only with your doctor's permission!

We're always moving against time but with nature, no matter what the condition of our bodies. Those of us who have muscular weakening or wasting disorders have to move with a little more effort to make progress, to stay in the same place, or sometimes just to lose what we have a little more slowly.

Don't waste time feeling sorry for yourself. It doesn't help at all. Time is precious! Use it well!

With your doctor's help, choose those areas in which the disease is most noticeable to you—those areas in which you are weakest. Select those exercises which will win you back some freedom to move in the world, and get started moving right away!

It is very, very important not to work to the point of exhaustion! Be sure to rest as often as you need to! If you can't do much without getting tired, do a little several times a day, and take naps or rest periods in between. Strengthen yourself slowly, but do it!

If you want to feel really good, keep a chart showing how many more exercises you can do each day! Make me feel good too! Send *me* a copy when you start making progress!

To get you up the stairs

EXERCISE	EASY	MEDIUM	HARD
3	√	√	
5	√		
6	√		√
8	√	√	
11	√		
20	√		

To get you up off the floor

EXERCISE	EASY	MEDIUM	HARD
14	√		
16	√		
29		√	
57	√	√	

To get you up out of chairs

EXERCISE	EASY	MEDIUM	HARD
20	√		
22	√	√	√

28	√	√	
29	√	√	
30		√	

To help you lift things

EXERCISE	EASY	MEDIUM	HARD
48	√	√	√
49	√	√	

To help you hold things

EXERCISE	EASY	MEDIUM	HARD
41		√	
42	√	√	
43	√	√	√

To keep you moving

EXERCISE	EASY	MEDIUM	HARD
1	√		
28	√		

To strengthen your abdominals

EXERCISE	EASY	MEDIUM	HARD
21	√		
22	√	√	√
28	√	√	

To strengthen your lower back

EXERCISE	EASY	MEDIUM	HARD
37	√		

Hernia

A hernia or "rupture" is the pushing out of any part from the cavity in which it normally belongs. You are not going to be able to get your body into the best possible condition if you have a hernia!

Sometimes you can tell whether you have one in your groin (which is the most common kind) by a number of hints from your body. You may get a small or large sharp pain in your groin when you laugh, cough, sneeze, or lift something heavy. If you do you should quickly and automatically press your hand to that area next time, before the strain, to try to prevent it doing more damage. You may actually be able to see a slight bulge in your groin when you either push hard, or sneeze, or cough. Whether you can see a bulge or not, if you have either pain or discomfort in this area, see a doctor!

To check yourself for a midline hernia, lie on your back on the floor, knees bent, feet on the floor, and lift your head up to your chest.

Most people have a clearly visible and perfectly natural line down the center of their belly. That center line *can part*. It tends to part rather high up (above your navel) but it can part further down also. If your belly comes up to a peak anywhere along that midline there is a chance that the connective fibers down your middle have parted. *If you have any of these signs do not attempt to do any abdominal exercises at all until you have been seen by a doctor!* If he finds that you do have a hernia, *do no abdominal exercises until you have had your hernia repaired!* Don't decide to ignore it! You won't be able to for long! See your doctor and follow his advice! And be sure to follow his advice about when to begin exercising after surgery! Don't start before he gives his permission!

When you do begin, do the very easiest of the abdominal exercises, no matter how strong you are otherwise! *Work up very slowly!*

After Surgery

After any surgery you will need periods of rest *and periods of movement!* Movement is necessary to help you heal faster and better. Movement also prevents adhesions—the sticking together of parts that should be free of each other. Movement gives you better circulation of blood, fewer chances for blood clots to form, and fewer chances for abnormal scar tissue to form. In general, an all-around faster, better recovery will come about with as early a return to movement as possible. You must, however, ask your doctor's advice!

Move on to other exercises according to what your surgery has been only with your doctor's approval and advice.

EXERCISE	EASY	MEDIUM	HARD
1	√		

Exercise 1 Easy is the most important.

EXERCISE	EASY	MEDIUM	HARD
22	√	√	
28	√		

THE EXERCISES

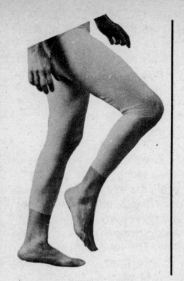

If you're weak, do the heel-toe walk the easy way:

Sit in a chair with your feet on the floor. ◊ Pick up one leg, then let it down, touching your toe to the floor first. ◊ Be sure your foot bends from the tip of your toes all the way down to your heel. ◊ Get as high up on the tip of your toes as possible!

If you're in good shape, do the standing version. Pull up a good sturdy chair to hold on to if you need it for balance.

Stand barefoot. ◊ Now start to walk in place, but do it by putting your toe down first and then your heel. ◊ Practice that movement slowly until you do it right every time. ◊ Then try speeding it up a little, day by day. ◊ Let go of the chair as soon as you feel you can safely.

FOOT OR LEG PROBLEMS? IT'S PROBABLY

ALL RIGHT TO DO THIS EXERCISE. BUT DO CHECK IT OUT WITH YOUR DOCTOR FIRST.

If you have one leg or foot that's weaker than the other, start from a sitting position in a chair and do only the weak leg for a while. When you feel the weak side getting a little better, try the standing position and gradually put more and more weight on your weak side until the legs and feet feel equally strong.

There are twenty-six bones in *each* foot. You want to exercise *all* the ligaments (connecting tissue that holds them together), strengthen all the muscles! This exercise is especially useful for strengthening your arches! If you are standing and walking, you are also improving the circulation of your blood, through your feet and legs and the rest of your body! Do your feet tend to get cold easily? Wear a pair, or two pairs, of socks—still no shoes—while you exercise, or even all the time that you're indoors. When it's really cold and my husband is away, I wear a pair to bed. Socks are comfortable, warm, healthful, and washable. You're warm, your feet can move naturally, the air can get to your feet, and you can wear fresh ones as often as you like! Try them! They're marvelous!

IMPORTANT! IF YOU ARE MORE OR LESS TRAPPED INSIDE BY THE WEATHER, YOUR HEALTH, YOUR FAMILY, OR ANYTHING ELSE, THIS EXERCISE ALONE CAN GET YOU INTO MUCH BETTER SHAPE, IF DONE CONSISTENTLY!

Bedridden? Put a rolled-up pillow at the foot of the bed and walk against it in a lying-down position.

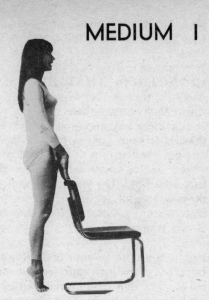

Stand barefoot.

Hold on to something sturdy when you first start this exercise—a chair, a sink, a bureau.

With your feet a little apart, go way up onto your toes and then come slowly down. ◇ Now you have some choices: you can go up and come down very slowly; you can go up and come down very fast; come down halfway and go up very slowly; come down halfway and go up very fast.

Do any of the variations using one foot, at a time, *while holding the other foot up off the floor!* See how long you can do any of the variations! See if you can do them without holding on! *Do them all barefoot, of course!*

If one of your feet or legs is weaker than the other, start the exercise sitting in a chair and using just the weak leg for a while. As you feel the foot beginning to improve, go to a standing position, but be sure not to favor the weak foot by using the strength of the strong foot to do most of the work! *Make that weak foot work!*

DO NOTHING THAT HURTS!

This exercise strengthens not only your arches and toes and ankles, but also your lower leg (from the knee down)! It helps your circulation and balance (as you'll find out the first time you let go)!

If you want a *larger* calf, you can come up on just one foot at a time. Do you know that when you come up on your toe, the foot is used in an entirely different way than when you wear heels? Want to see? Try it! Nobody's watching!

Put a high heel on one foot and leave the other bare. ◊ **Now put your weight on the foot with the shoe.** ◊ **Lean over and feel the calf of that leg— arch too, if you can.** ◊ **Now come up on the toe of the other foot and put your weight on that one, and lean over to feel the calf of that leg—and, again, the arch.**

Feel the difference? The arch of the foot in the shoe is being misused because it can relax in a position in which it should be working!

How much of the day do most women wear shoes? How long could you walk on your toes?

WALKING ON YOUR TOES IS GOOD WORK! WALKING IN HIGH HEELS IS RUIN! DOWN WITH HIGH HEELS!

Stand barefoot.

**Run in place lifting your feet right up off the floor.
◇ Put your toe down first and then lower your
foot on down to the heel. ◇ Make sure your heel
touches the floor each time! Pick your knees up
with each step! Tighten your bottom with each
step! Hold your belly in! Keep your chest up!
Keep your chin up! Breathe with your mouth
open! It is important only that you get the air in!**

Start slowly each day. Build up speed slowly each day.
Judge well how long you can run. And *slow down before stopping each day. That is very important.*
This has become one of my favorite "spare time" exercises. I use it while waiting for people, laundry, mail—
anytime I have a few spare minutes that might otherwise be wasted. Really great for telephone conversa-
tions!

If you have a space big enough to stand up in, you're
all set to keep in excellent shape! That's all it takes!

85

Toe–heel running in place is an all-weather, anytime, anywhere sport.

I like to wear lots of layers of warm clothing and really sweat!

Start slowly each and every day!

To relieve the boredom, turn on the T.V. and start the first day running with commercials. Work your way up over weeks or a month to running while watching movies. Television *can* be constructive! You can accomplish more indoors in a short time with this exercise than with almost any other (unless you add a jump rope to it)!

Pick up your knees higher yet! Come up higher on your toes! Let your heels touch the floor *each* time they come down!

Abilities unused become dis-abilities. *Circulation is the most important thing you have to work for!*

This exercise makes a great everyday habit! *A great way to relieve stress!* Something bothering you? Close yourself in a room and run as hard as you can. You'll feel better—honest!

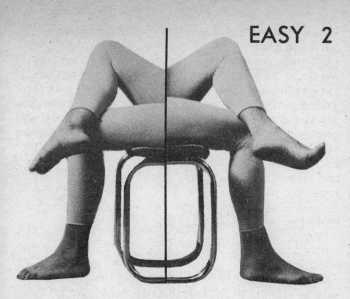

Sit in a chair or on the floor. ◊ **Cross one ankle or leg over the other.**

With the top foot, curl the toes under as far as possible and clench them. Then curl them back up and spread them out as much as you can. ◊ **Cross your legs the other way and do the same for the other foot.**

If you've been wearing shoes for a long time, and hardly ever run around barefoot, this exercise will feel strange to you. Your feet may either not seem able to understand what you want of them, or they may be very weak. Be patient with them, treat them well, keep trying, and they'll soon respond. Like someone who's been bedridden for a long time, they need care and understanding.

You may get cramps in them if you're not used to moving. Most of the cramps will occur in the bottom of your toes, or in your arches. If you do get a cramp, *don't leap around.* Stretch the toes as far up as you can with your hand or stand with your weight on that foot and you can most often stretch the cramp out.

For some reason, the cramps tend to come back, especially in the toes, after you think you are rid of them. If you're in your shoes and are embarrassed to take them off, and if your shoes will allow you, just put that foot behind you, toes bent forward and on the floor, and lean on them with some of your weight—as much as you need to relieve the discomfort.

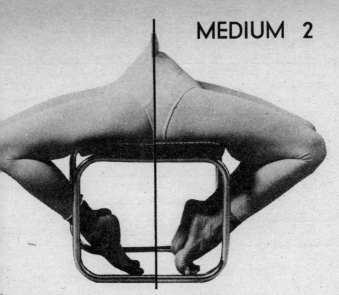

Sit in a chair. ◇ Curl the toes of both feet under as far as possible.

Then point the toes of one foot at a time and turn them way under to rest the tops of them on the floor under your chair. ◇ Bounce your knees down gently to help it along, once the feet are in place. ◇ To turn your toes in the other direction with some resistance, raise one foot and move it back until you're resting it on the bottom of your toes. ◇ (Don't let the ball of your foot touch the floor, if you can.) ◇ Then, the other foot. ◇ Bounce your knees gently forward and down to put on a little extra pressure.

NO FORCING! BE GENTLE!

In countries where people go without shoes, there are practically no foot problems at all! In shoe-wearing cultures, on the other hand, enormous numbers of people walk around (when they still can) with aching, uncomfortable, fungus-infected, corny, ingrown-toenailed, miserable feet. We limp; we stumble; we walk with our feet far apart; we hurt all over; we shift all our body lines trying to make our feet feel better. We pay enormous sums of money to doctors and hospitals for problems brought on because we're just too uncomfortable to move around any longer on our bad feet. *All we really need to do is take off our shoes!*

Do your feet "feel" terrible? Let them "feel" good! If you, right now, got rid of all shoes with heels of any sort, those made of materials that are not porous (that air can't get through), those that hold your foot rigid, that don't allow your foot to roll or your toes to spread, and began taking (after a slow buildup) an hour's walk every day, you could probably have happy, healthy feet again!

Get down on your knees on the floor. ◇ Point
your toes so that the tops of your feet lie along the
floor. ◇ Sit on your heels. ◇ Put your hands behind you on the floor for support.

Rock yourself back gently day by day, until your
knees will come up off the floor and you can rest
all your weight, without using your hands, on the
tops of your feet only. ◇ Try bouncing gently up
and down on your feet tops.

Get down on your knees on the floor. ◇ Sit on
your heels. ◇ Turn your toes so that the bottoms
of your toes are on the floor. ◇ Now try to rock
your knees a little forward, using your hands for
support as long as you need them. ◇ The farther
forward you can rock your knees, the farther your
toes will have to bend.

Hopefully by this time you stay barefoot as much of the
time as possible. Even if you do it only when at home,

it's going to be a big help—especially if you keep moving quite a bit. The longer you have allowed your feet to stiffen and sag in shoes, the longer it is going to take you to pull them back to flexibility and strength. But unless they are totally ruined it will happen, if you give them the time, the freedom, and the activity! And does it feel good!

In the exercise where you are resting on the tops of your toes, if you ever get so you feel comfortable without using your hands, try this:

Using your toe tops as a jumping-off point, but keeping them on the floor, come up with your bottom and your knees, and come down again. ◇ Try it first with your hands ready to lend support. ◇ When supporting yourself on the bottom of your toes, you can try going from a squat to a kneeling position, and then back. ◇ Use your hands to begin with, to give you extra support. ◇ When you can, pick your hands up off the floor and make your leg and foot muscles do the work.

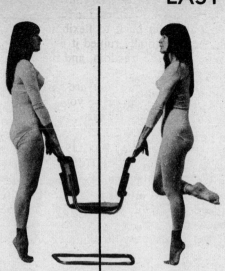

Stand barefoot.

Hold on to a bar, bureau, or the edge of a sink for support if you need to.

Come up onto the toes of both feet and then let your heels back down again.

Use your hands as much as you need to in the beginning. Do only once or twice the first day. When you can, use just light pressure from your fingers—or take them off the bar completely.

Go up and down very slowly. ◊ Go up and down very fast. ◊ Go up and down, not quite touching the floor with your heels, as many times as possible. ◊ Do the same thing (when you're able) using only one foot at a time.

Take your choice—or do them all!

93

Take off your shoes! How does it feel when you come up onto your toes? How does it feel to let your heels down to their natural level? Wiggle your toes around a little before you begin to exercise them. Get a little air between them. And a little light. And a little cool.

Kill the fungus!

Don't keep your socks on unless the floor is cold or has splinters. Naked feet can feel all kinds of things: heat, cold, sand, pebbles, rocks, carpets, concrete, other people's feet.

Have you ever tried to fold your toes as you do your hands? It's a lot of fun! Have you ever tried writing with a pen held in your toes? You really can!

Close your eyes and have someone put different things on the floor by your feet for you to identify, using *only* your feet. You'll be surprised just how sensitive they can be!

Don't put shoes on your children until you're forced to!

Stand on a folded washcloth so that the toes and front of one foot overlap it in front and the heel overlaps it in back.

Hold on to the back of a chair to steady yourself. Have your other foot on the floor for balance.

Come way up onto your toe and down to your heel again. Use less and less pressure from your hands as you feel steadier. Let go completely when you can safely. ◊ Go up and down slowly. ◊ Go up and down very fast. ◊ Be sure to touch your heels to the floor each time you come down. Be sure to come way up on tiptoe each time you go up. Keep your body upright—chest and chin up. ◊ Do the same thing with the other foot.

Doing this exercise on a folded washcloth is a little like walking on any uneven surface, such as grass, sand, or earth—your arch gets stretched a little differently from the way it does on a flat surface. Try putting a rolled or folded washcloth on a thick soft mat to make even more exercise for your foot. You can do the exercise with both feet at once if you want. A barefoot walk or run outside is better yet, but watch out for glass and metal scraps!

Be aware of how everything feels under your feet—how much farther your toes spread without shoes; how your foot rolls from the heel, along the outside of your foot, and up onto the ball of your foot to push off from the ball of your foot and your big toe into the next step. Unless you have an uncomfortable problem with walking, this action is usually automatic. Just for a new or renewed experience, feel the whole action.

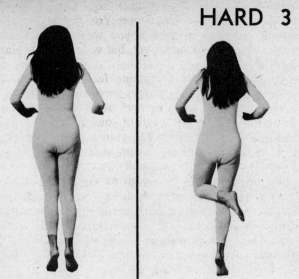

Stand barefoot.

Hold on to a bureau or the edge of a sink for support if you need to or if you're just beginning.

Using both feet, jump a little way off the floor and come down on your toes first and then lower to your heels, in a continuous movement. ◊ If your feet can take it, jump a little higher. ◊ When you can, lighten the pressure of your hands on the bar, until you can remove them altogether. ◊ Put your hands back on the bar when you first begin to do the jumping that uses only one foot at a time. You'll need the support! Remove them when or if you can. Be sure that your heels touch the floor every time!!

TAKE IT EASY! VERY GENTLY, IN THE BEGIN-NING.

Take it easy in the beginning. This exercise can really be hard on your arches. If your feet aren't already strong, you're in for a few aches and pains.

Jump very lightly to begin with. Not very far up and have a nice soft mat under your feet. Don't push it the first few days!

If you really accentuate the toe–heel movement in this exercise, you're going to feel it! It will make you a beautiful pair of arches, a beautiful pair of feet, a beautiful pair of legs, *and* good circulation and respiration. How's that for a great exercise?

Don't do too much or you'll be walking around with your toes curled up in cramps for the next week or so. And it hurts even worse in shoes—an arch ache!!

If you can be patient and persistent, you can have a gorgeous and comfortable and strong pair of feet and legs! Once you give them a taste of freedom and fun, though, they'll never be satisfied locked away again.

Give your feet their head.

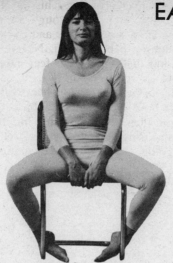

Sit in a chair. ◇ Turn your feet up on their outside edges, as far as possible, and keep them on those edges for the rest of the exercise.

Now see if, legs apart, you can put your feet behind the chair legs. ◇ Put first one leg out to the side and put your toes behind the leg of the chair on that side. ◇ Keep the side of your foot on the floor. Now do the same thing with the other foot. ◇ Try to bounce your heels up and down a little in this position, rocking forward.

Cramp? Stand up and put your weight on the cramped foot.

STRETCHING TAKES SLOW AND GENTLE MOVES. DON'T HURRY IT!

If, when you're standing with your toes pointed straight ahead, your ankles cave in toward each other, you have the wrong kind of flat feet and need this type of

99

exercise. It also is good just for making your feet more flexible.

If your feet ache a lot, it may be that you're standing still for too long a period of time. Your feet were not built to do that. They were built to move! The worst thing you can do to your feet is to stand for long periods of time, *in heels!* It's even worse if you're overweight! Your poor feet—first in splints, then held at a bad angle, and then made to weight-lift! It's no wonder they complain. Any ligament kept stretched is more than likely going to lose its natural bounce.

If you've got good feet and comfortable shoes, your feet will make your face smile!

Stand up with your legs a little apart. ◇ **Turn your toes way in.** ◇ **Turn your heels out as far as you can.** ◇ **Come up on the outside of your feet.**

Keep them in that position and walk. ◇ **Keep your back straight.**

IF ANYTHING HURTS, DO THE EASIER VERSION.

This is a weird position to walk around in, certainly not something you'd like to make an everyday walk out of, but it really is great for correcting flat feet.

You should do some of the toe–heel running or walking for a while first to get your feet good and flexible, so that your arch can develop properly. This is really important, because *arch supports are* not *going to make your arch strong again!* It would be like expecting a girdle to make your belly muscles strong!

Feet are not meant for standing, except for very short periods of time. *Feet are meant for movement!* If they're in such bad shape that you can't put too much weight on them, take off your shoes and rock in a rocking chair for a few weeks to give them a gentle push toward the right direction, and then get moving on them!

What have you got to do that you couldn't do better with better feet? Once your feet go, everything else *has* to follow. And if they don't go, sooner or later nothing else will! *Take good care of them!*

Stand up with your legs a little apart. ◇ **Turn your toes way in.** ◇ **Turn your heels as far out as you can.** ◇ **Come up on the outside of your feet.**

Keep them in that position and walk for a few minutes to warm up. ◇ **Now try running that way.** ◇ **Try jumping—but start with gentle jumping!**

Don't begin this exercise until you have been exercising your feet in lots of different ways for at least a couple of months. If you're used to walking a lot or you run or play any sport that keeps you moving on your feet, then, of course, you're all set.

The muscles underneath your foot work like a spring. They keep the arch from going too far down *if they're in good condition,* and they help the arch spring back up into more of an arch when you take your weight off the foot or feet. If the muscles and ligaments sag, so will your arches, and that's where a lot of troubles begin. The bones, muscles, ligaments, and so forth are all

103

dependent on one another. What's going to happen to your shock absorption if your springs are missing? *Keep that spring action! Keep moving!* People who can never stand still are healthier for it!

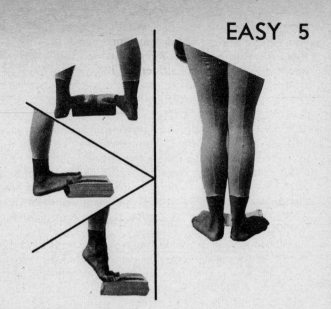

Stand barefoot. ◇ Put a catalogue or a two-inch-thick telephone book open side right up against the sink on the floor. ◇ Stand with your toes and the balls of your feet on either side of the book's spine with your heels turned out, and on the floor.

Use your hands for balance only, if you can—for support if you have to.

Lift your heels up as far as possible, coming up onto tiptoe on the book, and bring your heels slowly back down to the floor again. ◇ Move your heels a little farther toward each other and again come way up and down again. And a little farther toward each other and again way up and all the way down.

Try not to lean on the sink.

NO FORCING!

This exercise is going to stretch out and develop the backs of your legs and those muscles that help you to come up onto your toes. A lot of them are the same muscles. The front of the legs will be used too, but not as much as the backs.

Do you have trouble getting your heels down onto the floor when you walk? If you're used to wearing shoes with even a slight heel, and have trouble walking barefoot, even in the house, you probably need just this exercise to stretch the backs of your legs out.

There are quite a few muscles in the under part of your foot that serve to hold the foot in the proper position while you walk, unless you wear shoes! If you wear shoes, you have on a *splint* that prevents your foot from working normally!

We know a student (Émil) who went barefoot all one winter! He wore no shoes inside or out—even through snow and ice. He got used to it quickly, and was not a victim of chilblains or pneumonia. He has developed beautiful, healthy feet. I'm not suggesting—just relating.

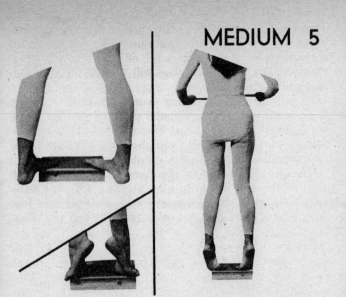

Stand barefoot. ◊ **Put a catalogue or a thick telephone book right up against the sink on the floor, open edge to the sink.** ◊ **Place your toes and the balls of your feet on the corners of the book's spine with your heels turned out, and on the floor.**

Use your hands on the sink for balance only, if you can —for support if you need to.

Keeping your toes and the balls of your feet in place, bring your heels up sharply to a tiptoe position, and immediately lower them to the floor again. ◊ **Move your heels only a little closer together and do it again. And a little closer, and do it again!** ◊ **Move all the way in and all the way out repeating the leap into tiptoe position and back down.** ◊ **Or see how long you can do it in one position before you move on to the next.**

Your arches, ligaments, and muscles in your feet are going to develop beautifully with this exercise. It may give you cramps in your feet, if you keep it up *too long* in the beginning, or cramps in the legs, the calves especially.

If you get a cramp in the calf, come down with your heel to the floor and raise your toes, and this position will stretch the cramp out. Quit for the day! Leaning forward against the sink will help get rid of it even faster.

Do you want strong and flexible feet and legs? You're going to get them with these exercises! You could add some running—in place if you must, but running forward will do a lot more for you if you need this exercise. The faster you run, the better! Make sure you work up to it first and make sure that you begin and end slowly every day.

If you're going to run in place, *be sure to bring your heel down to the floor each time* and to come way up onto your toe with the opposite foot.

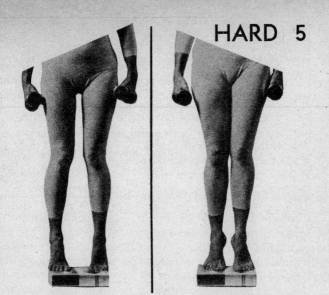

Stand barefoot. ◇ Put a catalogue or a thick telephone book on the floor as in the two easier exercises. ◇ Don't hold on to the sink this time! Use your arms to hold some weights, instead.

Work up gradually. You'll be surprised just how much you can hold and still do this! The more weight you work up to holding, the more work your feet and legs will be doing.

Place your toes and the balls of your feet on the back two corners of the book (at the bound edge) and with your heels turned out and touching the floor. ◇ Keeping your toes and the balls of your feet in place, bring your heels up slowly to a tiptoe position.

You want to be on tiptoe, not tipped over.

Then back down again. Once you're sure of yourself, bring your heels up fast. ◇ Slowly start to move your heels a little closer together, repeating the fast movement up and back down. ◊ Bring your heels closer. ◊ Either work your way in and out, or see how long you can do it in each position.

If you need feet that will stand a lot of extra stress and strain, for twisting and turning, pivoting and springing, jumping and anything else you can think of, you can build all these qualities in ahead of time, have them ready for work, by practicing this exercise.

If you want even *better* results, get out the exercises for the front of your legs and use them with this one.

This is an excellent conditioning exercise for sports. Conditioning should be a year-round activity, not just a seasonal one. You can keep yourself prepared for any sport, the year round, if you just pull out the exercises outlined in the "guide" and keep after them constantly. *And don't let the season of the sport itself interfere with the conditioning* (whether it be football or motherhood)! It takes just a little time to keep the conditioning at a peak level, constantly. In fact, it becomes very easy.

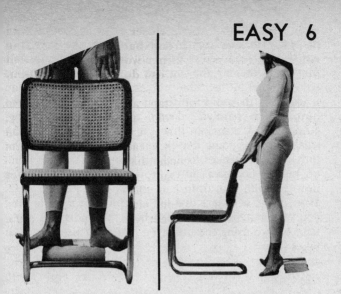

Stand barefoot. ◇ Put a catalogue or a thick book on the floor behind a sturdy chair, placing the back of the book, the spine, away from the chair. ◇ Face the chair, hold on to the back for support, and put your heels on the book at the opposite corners of the book's open end.

Raise your toes as high as possible and lower them to the floor again. ◇ Keeping your heels in place, continue to move your toes little by little in toward the center, raising and lowering them each time you move them in a little. ◇ Then slowly work your way back out so that your toes are pointing out to the sides again. ◇ Raise and lower them just as you did to bring them in.

All the muscles down the outside and the front of your lower leg work to pull your foot up from the front and the outside. Some of the muscles in the foot are helping out too.

Sometimes the problem known as "foot drop" can be

111

helped with exercises like this one. If the muscle is *really* paralyzed you've got a different job. It's possible that strengthening the muscles around it will help you to overcome most of the problem, but you may have to learn how to use your foot a little differently if you have a true paralysis. Don't give up without trying! Sometimes it turns out that a muscle is just weak, very weak, to the point that it seems paralyzed. It won't hurt to try exercises to make it stronger. You may end up being very pleasantly surprised! If you do have a problem with foot drop it is usually with just one foot. If so, work with just that leg and foot for a while until you've conquered or learned how to handle the problem, before using the other leg and foot. Be patient! It takes time.

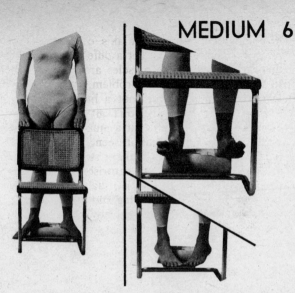

Stand barefoot. ◇ Put a catalogue or a thick book on the floor. ◇ Turn it so that you can read the title. ◇ Have a sturdy chair back in front of it. ◇ Stand with your heels on the top edge of the book at either corner. ◇ Hold on to the chair back for support as long as you need to, then shift to just using light pressure from your fingertips for balance.

Raise your toes as high and as quickly as possible and then lower them. ◇ Keeping your heels in place, continue to move your toes in toward the center, raising and lowering them very fast, each time you move a little farther in. ◇ Continue to raise and lower them quickly as you move little by little back to your original position.

If the muscles in the front and sides of your legs are pretty good but you want better ones, this is the way to get them. You could also jump rope, climb, or hop, skip, and jump your way into better leg muscles in general. Or you could ride a bike, paddle a boat (with your feet), walk a lot, dance, or run.

Believe it or not, these exercises can make your legs ache! Nothing serious. It feels good when you know that you're aching from exercising. It feels even better if you know that you're aching from dancing!

Don't just "live a little"; live a lot!

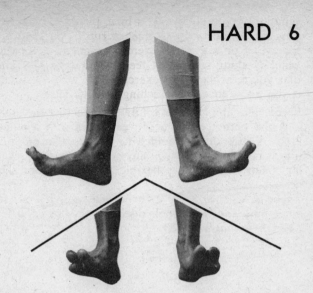

**Stand with your legs a little way apart. ◇ Hold on
to something if you need to. ◇ Turn your toes
out as far as you can.**

**Try to lift them up as high as you can and lower
them to the floor again. ◇ Keeping your heels in
place, continue to move your toes just a little way
at a time in toward the center, raising and lowering
them each step of the way. ◇ Then move them
little by little back out to the sides again, still raising and lowering them. ◇ Keep your bottom from
sticking out!**

You have to get down off the books for the hard part.
The hardest few inches to raise your feet are the top
few. Try it and see.

Here is something interesting to look for: did you know
that an arch in the very best condition will flatten to
some extent when you put your body weight on it?
Maybe it won't flatten out to touch the ground completely, but it is very flexible and gives a great deal

under your weight. When your weight is off it, it will arch up again. A flexible arch gives you a lot of bounce! An inflexible arch, which stays cramped up high, is not going to do you much good if you jump from a tree, or even a curb.

Shoes with arches built in can ruin perfectly good feet. If your feet and legs don't hurt you, whether the arches look flat or not, don't ever wear shoes with a built-in arch! A shoe that is molded to your foot in one position is not going to do you any good when you're walking. Your feet are very flexible. So should your shoes be!

There is no such thing as a normal foot. If your feet don't hurt and don't look diseased, they're good feet. *Keep them that way! Move!*

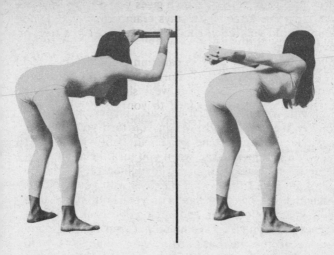

Stand with your knees a little apart. ◇ Hold on to
a bureau or a sink. ◇ Stick your bottom out. ◇
Arch your back. ◇ Keep your head up. ◇ Bend
your knees a little.

Bounce up and down a little using both your bottom and your knees. ◇ When you can do that
very easily, stand away from the support. ◇ Clasp
your hands behind your back. ◇ Keep the rest of
your body in the original position and bounce up
and down a little. When it's easy, bounce lower and
harder.

NOT FOR BAD BACKS!

You deserve to have a good bottom and back and
thighs. This exercise is a good beginning and could do
the whole job by itself if you don't want to go any
further.

To make it better for all the underlying muscles of the

bottom and for the inner and outer thighs, try these variations.

To get your inner thighs, put your legs a little farther apart and turn your toes in. ◊ **Now jump for a while in that position.** ◊ **To get your outer thighs, with your legs still a little apart turn your toes out and again jump in that position.**

Feel with your hands what happens to your thighs when you try these variations. When you turn your toes in, the inner thighs become good and tight—and tighter yet when you jump! And when you turn them out, your outer thighs become tighter and tighter yet when you jump! Be sure to feel what happens with your bottom. Straighten up; put your hands on your bottom and then stick your bottom out and arch your back. Big difference? Straighten up again and put your hands around your waistline in back with your thumbs toward each other; then stick your bottom out again and arch your back. With that kind of a difference in the use of the muscle, don't worry if you have to keep holding on to a support for a while.

Stand with your feet a little apart. ◊ Stick your bottom out. ◊ Arch your back up, to bring you parallel to the floor. ◊ Keep your head up. ◊ Clasp your hands behind your back.

Jump lightly off the floor. ◊ Keep your arms held up as high as possible. Try to keep your back parallel to the floor. Jump a little longer each day. ◊ When you can, try jumping with your hands clasped behind your back. Keep your head up! Try to keep your back parallel to the floor. ◊ When you can, try it with your arms stretched out in front of you at chin level.

Remember, though, that your back stays arched (look in a mirror) and your head stays up.

THIS EXERCISE IS NOT FOR BAD BACKS! IT IS ALSO NOT FOR BAD KNEES!

It won't do any good if you can't keep your back arched and head up. Go back to an easier exercise if it's too hard. Nobody's looking! Your pride may suffer, but that's better than your back!

You can work your way up very quickly. As you get better you can jump higher and higher, but try to keep your back almost parallel to the floor and your arms in the proper position. The harder you jump, the more you're going to use the muscles.

Put a rug under your feet if you're doing this exercise at home. It's a little quieter. A rubber-backed rug, please, so it won't slip! Don't do too many to begin with. A stiff bottom really feels strange.

If you want to work on your inner thighs especially, do this exercise a lot with your toes turned in. Outer thighs? Do a lot with your toes turned out. Thigh fronts? Keep your knees straight ahead.

Stand with your feet a little apart. ◇ Stick your bottom out. ◇ Arch your back up to bring your back almost parallel to the floor. ◇ Keep your head up. ◇ Have a small weight between your hands. Clasp your hands behind your back.

Jump very lightly off the floor—test yourself with the weight. ◇ When you can, extend your arms straight back. ◇ Keep your back parallel to the floor.

Make sure when you jump that you don't let the weights fall to hit you in the back. Keep a tight hold!

When you can, try jumping with the weights held behind your head, right against the back of your neck! ◇ Use one larger weight instead of two small ones whenever possible. ◇ When you can (and this is hard!), try it with the weights held out in front of you at chin level.

BE CAREFUL! TAKE THIS ONE VERY EASY! START WITH VERY LIGHT WEIGHTS.
IF YOU'RE GOING TO CHANGE THE POSITION OF YOUR FEET AND KNEES (OUT FOR OUTER THIGHS—IN FOR INNER THIGHS) TEST IT SLOWLY FIRST!

This should give you a beautiful bottom!

It can really be a strain on the back, so take your time and start with light weights. Work your way up very slowly. Don't attempt those last two variations without testing them first.

You can do yourself a lot of good in a hurry with these, *if you're careful! You can do a lot of damage, if you're not!*

Besides building up with the weights, you can increase how high or how fast you jump.

Keep everything under control, especially on the last step!

If you're going to do this exercise somewhere in the house, make it either the first floor or the basement. It can get pretty noisy!

Keep any weights other than bean bags, which are great and safe for the kids, out of the reach of young children. They can be very dangerous. If you're using adjustable weights, be sure to tighten them up every day before you use them. (They can be very dangerous for adults too!)

TEST THE TWO VARIATIONS IN THE EXERCISE ALL OVER AGAIN, EACH TIME YOU INCREASE THE WEIGHTS.

Sit on the edge of a chair and try these.

This exercise has four parts. Don't miss any.

1. Put your feet together. ◊ Let your knees fall apart, left hand against the inside of the right knee. ◊ Bounce the knee gently out. Do the same thing with the right hand on the left knee.

2. Place your feet apart, your knees almost together. ◊ Put your right hand against the right knee on the outside, left hand on the outside of the left knee. ◊ Bounce your knees in gently toward the floor.

3. Stretch your legs straight in front of you to rest on your heels. ◊ Put your hands on your knees, and gently bounce your knees in toward the floor.

4. Lift one leg up from the sitting position, knee bent. ◊ Put both hands around the front of the calf. ◊ Try to pull the lower leg in as close to your thigh as possible. ◊ Do the same movement with the other leg.

KNEES ARE VERY DELICATE! IF YOU HAVE BAD KNEES, DON'T DO ANY EXERCISES WITHOUT THE ADVICE OF YOUR DOCTOR!

What you want to do in this exercise if you have knee problems is to make as many moves as possible without causing pain. It is very important to keep moving! If you let your knee rest too long when it's in trouble you are more than likely going to make it worse rather than better. When the doctor says you may begin to use it again, after either an injury or an arthritic attack, or if you have just been inactive over a very long period of time, be sure to *begin slowly*.

Knees do an amazing job, an amazing *number* of jobs. They support, balance, absorb shock. There is so much going on at the knees that it's little wonder we have so many problems with them. And since the stress comes from all directions—front, back, and both sides—and since we cannot move around very well without them, they are worthy of all the attention we can give them.

Knees are weakest to the sides! *Be very gentle with the sideways movements when you first begin!* Always begin with gentle flexibility movements.

GENTLY!

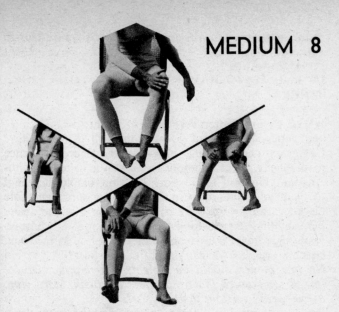

Sit on the edge of a chair.

1. Feet together. ◇ Let your knees fall apart, left hand against inside of right knee. ◇ Push the knee in steadily as you resist with your hand until your knee is upright.

2. Put your feet apart, your knees almost together. ◇ Put your right hand against the outside of your right knee, your left hand against the outside of your left knee. ◇ Press steadily out with your knees while resisting with your hands until your knees are upright.

3. Stretch your legs out straight in front to rest on your heels. Place both hands on one knee. ◇ Pull your heel steadily in against resistance from your hands. ◇ Do the same with the other leg.

4. Lift one leg up, knee bent. ◇ Put both hands under that knee, and push it steadily down with re-

sistance from your hands. ◇ **Do the same thing with the other leg.**

IF YOU HAVE BAD KNEES, ASK YOUR DOCTOR!

Knees are quite often very hard to repair; it takes time and patience! Why put yourself through it needlessly? Get your knees in the best possible shape, slowly, methodically, gently, before any strain is called for.

Anyone going out for a sport, dancing, or physical activity of any kind really ought to make sure first that his knees are in the very best condition that they can be. Anything less is foolish! They are the only knees you'll ever have! How many athletes do you know who become cripples when trying to climb stairs?

No first moves should be violent, or overdone! Don't take it for granted that your knees are okay. Start with the very easy versions first!

Do you think I'm overdoing the warnings? Anyone who has bad knees knows I'm not. Ask around. Find someone who has bad knees; it won't be hard. Ask him what it's like.

Stand barefoot.

1. **Heels together.** ◊ Lean over, put your hands on the inside of the opposite knees. ◊ Push your knees far apart and then pull them back together again with resistance the whole time from your hands.

2. **Put your feet apart.** ◊ Lean over and put your hands on the outside of your knees. ◊ Push your knees in and pull them back out with continued resistance from your hands.

3. **Lean over to put both hands on the top of one knee.** ◊ Pull your knee up as far as possible and then push it all the way down, keeping pressure against your hands the whole way. ◊ Then do the same with the other leg.

4. **Lean over to put both hands around under one knee.** ◊ Pull your knee all the way up and then

push it all the way down against steady pressure from your hands. ◊ **Do the same thing with the other leg.**

BE SURE TO KEEP BREATHING NORMALLY! DON'T HOLD YOUR BREATH! BAD KNEES? ASK YOUR DOCTOR!

No one, no matter how good you think your knees are, should start with this exercise! Work your way up from the beginning exercises, even if you think you don't need it. *It takes just one second to ruin a knee for a lifetime!* This is a great strengthening and stretching exercise for your knees. While one part of the knees is being tightened the other side is being stretched. Done under control, it is great practice and a great conditioner for those sports that call for all kinds of twisting and bending motions of the knee.

If you learn how to move right, *under control,* it is always much easier in an unexpected situation, such as in football or hockey, to have your knees hold up and come through safely (in the meantime doing an even better job of whatever is expected of them). It would be nice to have a bunch of healthy, whole ex-athletes or, rather, it would be nice if they could choose when to quit, rather than being forced to.

WARNING! EASY DOES IT—AND DOES IT BETTER!

Squat on the balls of your feet and put your hands on the floor in front of you.

Keeping your hands on the floor, bounce your bottom gently up and down.

If you aren't used to bending your knees lower than to sit in a chair, look in the "guide" for an even simpler bending exercise.

THIS EXERCISE IS NOT FOR BAD KNEES!

Easy? It was meant to be. Even so, if you haven't bent your knees this far for a long time it is not the exercise for you.

To improve rather than to ruin yourself, don't do this exercise if you have any trouble at all with your knees when you're in this position. If you get anything more than slight catches every now and then when you climb or lift and carry heavy articles, check with your doctor before doing *any* knee exercises. Your doctor can guide you in which exercises would be best for you or send you to someone who can.

After you can do this exercise for any length of time, be sure to straighten up every now and then and jump around a little to restore your circulation.

Anyone who is used to moving a lot can sit in this position for long periods of time with no problems whatsoever. But those people, ordinarily, would not need this easy an exercise.

Squat on the balls of your feet. ◊ **Put your hands out in front or off to each side for balance.**

Jump, bringing your feet a little up off the floor.

In the beginning, do this exercise just a few times. Build up slowly. If you feel yourself losing your balance, put your hands down for just a second to catch yourself and continue.

THIS EXERCISE IS NOT FOR BAD KNEES!

This exercise will use the same muscles that you use to sit on the floor or to squat; it will just use them a little more vigorously.

Keeping your hands off the floor while you're in motion will also improve your balance.

The movement works pretty well on the big front-of-the thigh muscle, the rectus femoris, which, translated, means, "Direct along the femur." (The femur is the big thigh bone, the largest bone in the body.)

The knee is obviously also going to get a lot of stretching along with the muscle developing. *Again, be careful of your knees!* Work your way through the easy version of the exercise first—*after* working your way through the yet easier exercises for the knees that you'll find in the "guide."

Since your arms are free on this one, you can find out for yourself what's working: feel your legs all the way up and down while you're jumping. Front, back, inside the thigh, outside, your calf, front of your lower leg, ankle, even your feet! Feel your back up under your rib cage. It's really a beautiful body you've got working for you. Everything works together.

If you jump for a long time (*after* you're in good shape) until you get tired, and then close your eyes, you can feel the muscles working.

DON'T OVERDO!

Squat. ◊ **Arms overhead, elbows straight, arms tight to ears.**

Jump, bringing your feet well off the floor.

Are you pretty good at that?

Jump along the floor. ◊ **Jump with your eyes closed.** ◊ **Jump up to a standing position and jump down.** ◊ **Jump side to side.** ◊ **Jump in a circle and then in the other direction.** ◊ **Jump in circles with your eyes closed.** ◊ **Jump side to side with your eyes closed.** ◊ **Jump backwards.** ◊ **Jump backwards with your eyes closed.**

DO THESE EXERCISES ONLY AFTER YOU HAVE DEVELOPED EXCELLENT KNEES! DON'T TAKE CHANCES!

Are you really in top shape? Do all these variations one after the other without a rest.

133

In all kinds of competitive sports you need to have *excellent* knees! It is far better to get them into the best shape *before* you start beating on them or getting them beat on, from all sides. The most common knee injuries in sports occur from twisting the knees and especially from their being hit from the sides.

Don't put all of your time in on these jumping exercises. Go to the exercises meant to get your knees into shape from all angles.

Knees are precious!

If you're in a competitive sport, they are worth all the time you can put in to build them. If you don't build them, you have only yourself to blame for problems. If you do build them, you can blame the people who hit you. That's a lot more satisfying.

Stand barefoot. ◇ **Hold on to a bar, a bureau, or a sink.**

Whatever it is, make sure it's sturdy and steady.

Put the left leg back behind you and slowly lower yourself by bending the right knee, to put the left knee on the floor. ◇ **Use your hands on the bar to help you come back up if necessary.**

Use a pillow under the back knee if your knees are at all delicate or sensitive. Go just a little way down and back up if it's too tough!

Do the same thing, letting the left knee bend, to lower the right leg, which is behind you, to put the right knee on the floor. ◇ **Do first one leg and then the other.** ◇ **As you get stronger, do more times on each side before shifting to the other.** ◇

As you get stronger try to use the bar less and less, until you can do without it.

DON'T DO THIS EXERCISE AT ALL IF YOUR KNEES ARE BAD!

Try not to lean forward as you come back up from the floor. Make sure that you cross the back leg slightly behind the front one as you put it back. This works the inner thigh a little better.

If you get down and find that you can't get back up, bring the other knee down too and use your hands on the floor to help yourself back up. Don't worry about it. You have to start someplace. Continue to let yourself down the right way and then crawl up, until you're strong enough to come back up the right way.

The more slowly you let yourself down, the right way, the sooner you'll be strong enough to get up the right way. You could also try going just part way down and coming back up again. Each time you do it try to go a little lower before you start back up.

Even if you just go a little way down, you're doing a lot of good for your inner thigh, and if that's all you can do, you really need this exercise.

Joggle your inner thigh with your hand. Do you want to leave it that way?

Stand barefoot.

Cross one foot in front of the other and come down onto the back knee. ◊ **Holding your head and your back up straight the whole time, come back up to a standing position. "No hands!"** ◊ **Walk along the floor this way, using first one foot and then the other.**

NOT FOR BAD KNEES!

Don't begin this exercise until you can come up and down from the floor in one place without hanging on with your hands.

Remember to keep your back as straight as possible. Also your head! Now very gracefully and elegantly walk along the floor by crossing one leg far across the other and lowering yourself onto the back knee.

It's not fair to get back up by putting your hands on the floor! If you can't accomplish it "no hands," go back to the easier exercise.

137

This one really lets you know the next day if you've done too many!

START THE FIRST DAY CAUTIOUSLY. DO THE EXERCISE JUST ONCE! IF YOU'VE GOT BAD KNEES, LEAVE IT ALONE!

If you learn to lift correctly and do a lot of lifting, you will automatically have good inner thighs. Lifting from the floor correctly means you must squat to the floor, pull the object in close, and then rise. *This will also protect your back from accidents!*
Most back accidents come from lifting things the wrong way.

Stand barefoot.

Cross the right leg over the left and lower yourself to the floor.

If you just fell to the floor, go back one exercise.

If you landed safely, pick up the right foot and place it across the other thigh to rest on the floor, with your toes near your left knee. ◊ **Without using your hands, lift yourself forward off your bottom and come up by rolling first onto your left knee and then rising.** ◊ **Do the same thing, crossing the left leg over.** ◊ **When you're strong enough, come forward and up without rolling onto the knee. Just lift with the side of one foot and the bottom of the other.**

Hard! Easy? Continue coming up and down for a while, without stopping. Do to the other side too!

NOT FOR BAD KNEES, PLEASE!

Your thighs have to be in pretty good shape for you to be able to do this at all.

If you sat on the floor all the time, you probably would never need this as an extra exercise. I mean, of course, if the floor was where you sat, when you did sit. If you sat there all the time, you would very soon not be able to stand without help.

Do you want good inner thighs with little or no effort? Just get into the habit of sitting on the floor. And when you rise, *don't use your hands!* Good "all-over" exercise for the inner thighs is rope climbing. Look at the thighs of circus rope climbers! Just look at the climbers in general! The whole body! You'll see a healthy body. An alert body. And a beautiful one. Maybe you could just hang a rope up in the back yard, but you won't have as much fun as the circus climbers. You should hang one up for the kids, anyway. It will save them a lot of problems later.

Being active is a habit. Kinds of activity are also a habit. What they enjoy now they will enjoy later—*if you encourage it!*

The best way to encourage is to set an example.

Stand at arm's length from a sink or a bureau, feet apart. ◊ Place your hands on the edge; get a good grip.

Let your knees in to touch and lower them as much as possible. ◊ Come back up. ◊ As you get better at this movement, try to let your knees go all the way to the floor. ◊ Use your arms for a while if you need to, to help yourself back up.

NOT FOR BAD KNEES!

The less pressure you use from your hands the more you're going to work the front and side of your thighs. Be sure you don't let go of the support until you feel entirely secure doing so. Just use less and less pressure as you become stronger.

This movement exercises the *vastus lateralis,* or "large side" muscle, and, in addition, the long strip of connective tissue running down the length of the thigh, from the top of the pelvis to below the knee, and the small muscle attached at the top and front of that connective tissue that keeps it pulled up tight (if it's in good condition). This move also gets the "quadriceps." This is not a set of exercises that needs to be practiced constantly unless you are in training for sports. If greater knee flexibility and strength is going to be needed for sports, start *a few months early* to build it! Don't wait! This is an important part of good training!

NOT FOR BAD KNEES! SORRY!

Stand barefoot.

Place soft pillows all around you or, better yet, use a very thick mat on the floor.

Put your feet apart, arms out anywhere you need them for balance.

Bend your knees toward each other and lower them to the floor; they should end up side by side. ◇ From this position on the floor, try to lift yourself back up to a standing position without shifting your feet. ◇ Use your hands a little to get you started at first, if you have to. ◇ Stop using your hands as soon as you can.

WARNING! NOT FOR BAD KNEES!

You *do* need good knees for this one and a certain amount of strength to let yourself down without a thump and back up without using your hands. If it's too tough you should always go back a step! How about just using your hands to help you get back up, and going down without help—if you can?

These are the muscles that give you smooth sides and front to your thigh. So-called saddlebags are, for some curious reason, mostly a female problem. But men can be quite weak in this area also.

When you first try this exercise at least have something handy to grab if you feel yourself losing strength fast. You could really hurt your knees if you let yourself down too hard. *That could set you back a while!*

Always take *all* precautions possible to protect yourself from injury! It's pretty embarrassing to admit that you hurt *yourself!* We all do it every now and then, though. Protect your knees! They're hard to repair.

Stand with your feet just a little apart. ◇ Put your hands where you need them for balance. ◇ Better yet, hold on to something solid until you don't need to any more.

Jump your feet apart as you let your knees come down on soft pillows or a mat. ◇ Use control so that your knees don't ever come down with a bang! ◇ Jump right back up again, bringing your feet a little closer together.

Take care! Be aware of what you're doing every second!

OLD KNEE INJURIES? BEWARE.

You have to be really aware of your abilities before beginning this exercise. Be sure that you have practiced the easy or medium version long and well before attempting this.

IF YOU HAVE EVER HAD A KNEE INJURY— EVER—DON'T DO THIS WITH ANYTHING LESS THAN EXTREME CAUTION!

If you feel any catches in your knees while doing it, go back to an easier version until you no longer feel any discomfort at all, ever, while doing that one, and then come back and try again. *Please!*

These exercises should always be done with your mind fixed on what you're doing. Don't fool around!

Don't do too many to begin with. One is plenty. Build up slowly.

This exercise is really only for people who want to be in *top condition!* It's hardly necessary for us ordinary people. Great for athletes!

Another safety factor! If your condition is excellent you will be less likely to injure yourself in a game.

AGAIN, THIS IS NOT FOR BAD KNEES!

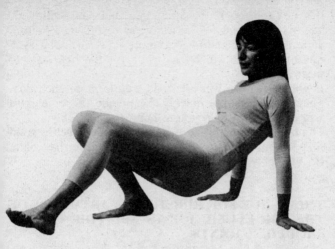

Sit on the floor. ◊ Knees bent. ◊ Feet on the floor. ◊ Hands resting on the floor behind you.

Lift your bottom up off the floor. ◊ Walk along on hands and feet, first forward and then backward.

DO YOU HAVE SHOULDER PROBLEMS? GO CAREFULLY, IF AT ALL! DOES ANYTHING HURT? GO BACK TO WORKING SEPARATE PARTS.

If this is difficult for you when you are first beginning, with your hands and feet on the floor, just try to raise and lower your bottom. If it's too difficult to do from the floor, do it from a chair.

Keep it up, day after day, until it becomes easy and then go on to the walking part.

If you find it difficult to walk backward, just do it forward for a while. If you find it difficult to walk forward, just walk backward for a while. *Anything* that helps to get you on your way is fine!

If it's *all* too tough, try sitting in a chair and, with your hands on the seat or the arms, try to lift your bottom up a little. Raise and lower it more times each day. Any rate of speed at which *you* can go is the *right* rate of speed.

If your arms are weak just do a *little* more each day. They will build very quickly. You could do some extra arm exercises to help you to build more quickly.

The backs of the thighs are very difficult to get in good shape. This exercise will start you along the right path. Be sure of your strength with this exercise before you go on.

THIS IS NOT FOR BURSITIS OR ARTHRITIS OF THE SHOULDER JOINTS OR FOR FROZEN SHOULDER JOINTS.

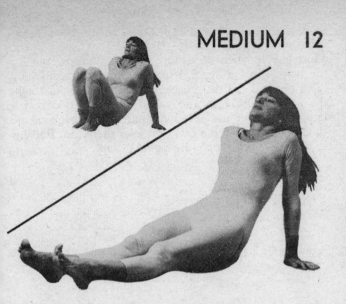

Sit on the floor, with your knees bent and your hands resting on the floor behind you.

Lift your bottom up and keep it up while you jump your feet way out as far as you can and back in as far as you can. ◊ Don't let your bottom touch the floor at all!

DO YOU HAVE BAD SHOULDERS? BAD KNEES? BEWARE! GO BACK TO EASIER EXERCISES.

Now you're really beginning to use the backs of the thighs.
Do it just a few times to begin with.
If you get enthusiastic (I always do) and end up with a cramp in the back of your thigh, sit down quickly, straighten out your legs, and lean over them to try to put your hands over your toes. That should stretch out the cramp.
If you've once given yourself a cramp, you're not going

149

to be able to do any more of the same for the day. Go on to something else.

Most people when they think of their "biceps" picture the muscle in the upper arm. But "biceps" means only "two heads," and the muscle in the back of your thigh, the major muscle, is also called "biceps." It covers a large portion of the outermost part of the back of the thigh. There are some other muscles there too. But this is the one most people are familiar with.

Sit on the floor, with your knees bent, feet on the floor, your hands resting on the floor behind you.

Lift your bottom off the floor. ◊ Raise your left leg and rest it on the right knee as you jump your right leg out as far as you can and then back in as far as you can. ◊ Do the same thing with the left leg. ◊ Try jumping in and out with one leg as long as you can. ◊ Then try it with the other.

FOR THIS YOU HAVE TO HAVE GOOD KNEES AND SHOULDERS!

This exercise is a good one!
When you can, hold your free leg out in midair. It's just a *little* harder that way. See how many times you can do it with each leg. See how fast you can do it with each leg. How long and how fast can you do it with each leg? This movement really does a lot for your *entire* body, but basically it's for improving the backs of your thighs. Add some of the exercises that have your arms more

151

active while holding up your body weight, such as jumping push-ups, or some such thing.

Don't neglect any one part unless it is already in *very* good condition and you're trying to even up the rest of your body to match, or if you need it in the best condition possible for a special purpose. Try to have all parts of your body in *equally* good condition! If possible move all at once from "easy" exercises to "medium," from "medium" to "hard" exercises.

quat, heels flat on the floor. ◊ Put your legs a
tle apart. ◊ Place your hands flat on the floor
tween your legs.

ounce your bottom up and down as far as pos-
le. ◊ Turn to put both hands on the floor at
e outside of your right foot. ◊ Bounce your bot-
m up and down as far as possible. ◊ Turn to
t both hands on the floor at the outside of your
ft foot. ◊ Bounce your bottom up and down as
r as possible.

YOU HAVE BAD KNEES, DON'T DO IT!

hen you first begin, you may have trouble keeping
ur heels down. See if it isn't easier with your feet and
gs farther apart.
you have trouble with your knees, it is obviously not
e exercise for you.
hen you first begin you may also have to rest very
ten. That's not surprising!

This is a good exercise for the thighs and you're going to feel it very quickly.

Don't do too many to begin with and even after you've been doing them for a while, take a break every now and then and do something different.

It'll get your bottom, too.

You don't need to feel what you're doing with your hands. If you do just a few too many, you'll feel it tomorrow without any help from your hands. Never worry about getting stiff. It's good for you! And if you get *too* stiff, there's always the hot bath. Sitting on a stiff bottom, even in a hot bath, is not the most comfortable feeling in the world. You could say, though, that it's sensational! Miserably so!

Squat, heels flat on the floor, legs far apart. ◊ Put your hands flat on the floor between your legs.

Keeping your hands on the floor the whole time, jump, bringing only your feet up off the floor and back down. ◊ Get them up as high as possible, but be sure to come down each time flatly on your feet. ◊ Put both hands to the right side of your right foot and try it again. ◊ And to the left side of your left foot and try it again.

IF YOU HAVE BAD KNEES, DON'T DO THESE. LOOK IN THE "GUIDE"!

These movements put a little more muscle into your work. They develop the backs of your thighs, and also the backs of your calves.

IF YOU HAVE ANY TROUBLE WITH YOUR KNEES AT ALL, LEAVE THE EXERCISE ALONE.

DON'T CONTINUE ANY EXERCISE THAT GIVES YOU PAIN, EVER!

If this exercise bothers you but the easier one didn't, go back.

One of the larger muscles you're getting here is the large bottom muscle called the *gluteus maximus*. The name comes from the Greek *gloutos*, meaning "rump," and the Latin *maximus*, meaning "largest." Putting them together, it means "largest rump muscle." Too often a "fitting" description.

Then there is the "little rump muscle" and the "medium rump muscle."

And, of course, there are all the others down the sides of the thighs, inside and out, and those down the front and back of the thighs. You get all of these muscles at once with these jumps.

Don't do too many the first day! You build fast with these!

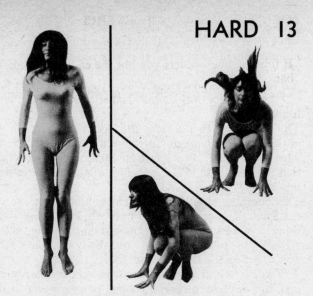

Stand barefoot, with your knees apart.

You must have very good knees even to begin this!

Without jumping at first, slowly squat down to make sure your feet are far enough apart so that you can come down and lower your heels flat on the floor. ◊ Keep them in place and stand again.

Now begin the exercise. Watching where your feet are placed, jump up and come down into a squat, lowering your heels to the floor. ◊ Keep it up, jumping both up and down. ◊ Always bring your hands down to touch the floor in front of you. ◊ Now try the same thing (always testing first) but placing both hands to the side of one foot. ◊ Then try it with both hands coming down to the floor at the side of the other foot.

THIS EXERCISE IS ONLY FOR THE BEST KNEES!

This one's a pip! All by itself it can wear you out for a while. But it's worth it. It leaves beautiful, tight, elastic muscle behind (and down the sides and the front).

If you get any kinks in your knees doing it, *don't go any further. Quit!* Go back one, where your knees don't have to take so much of the work, and stick with that a while longer.

The variations to the sides are also very good for the muscles and ligaments surrounding the knees. That's why you should always test an exercise first. Anything that can help you is also capable of hurting you if done unwisely.

This jumping should be a great conditioning exercise for football, soccer, hockey, baseball, swimming—anything, everything—dancing, mountain climbing, skiing. Always be aware of what your body is doing while you're practicing this exercise.

The knees are at a slight disadvantage in this exercise and you must keep careful control of your movements.

I still say "bouncy moves" make "bouncy looking" muscles, and that's how good thighs look—"bouncy"!

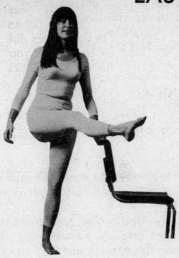

Stand barefoot.

Put twelve pieces of paper, each one marked with a number from one to twelve, in a circle around you on the floor, like a clock. Twelve o'clock straight ahead and six o'clock behind you and so on. Have a chair back at your side to hold on to for support. Start with the chair on your left.

Swing your right leg very gently toward ten o'clock just once and back (let it swing loosely) and then swing it toward eleven, twelve, one, and so on. ◊ When you get to three, swing it across in front of you and over to three. ◊ Do the same gentle, loose swinging motion all the way around until your leg is swinging toward eight behind you. ◊ Now put the chair on the other side of you and use the other leg. ◊ Start the left leg swinging toward two o'clock and work your way all the way around again.

If you feel any discomfort at all, move around that point and go on. If it doesn't bother you, increase the number of times you swing toward each number each day. Don't push it! Stop if you get tired. You've got lots of time. Breathe normally! *Don't hold your breath.*

This one can be hard on back problems too!

If you're having trouble with your lower back, have the non-swinging foot on a stool or catalogue. Hold on tight. Swing very gently.

HIP JOINT PROBLEMS? HANDLE VERY GENTLY.

For loosening up stiff hips, there is nothing better.

If any move bothers you, just *don't* swing as far in that direction!

If you have arthritic hips, you might try taking a hot bath and then dressing warmly before beginning.

Anyone who has one leg slightly shorter than the other can, quite often, appear to even it with the other with just this simple exercise, and to all intents and purposes, make it a normal-length leg. If that is a problem with you, stand with the longer leg on a thick book or catalogue and swing the shorter leg. In general treat that leg to more of these flexibility exercises. Be sure to go on to the other variations, slowly, but do go on. If your problem is extreme enough, you may need the addition of the weight in the last variation to do the trick. Once you get used to the exercise you certainly won't need to keep putting the paper clock around you.

Any kind of hip injury should not be allowed, after the first recovery period, to rest. Injured joints tend to "freeze" or not be able to get full motion back. If you work at it, quite often you *will* get full motion back!

Stand barefoot.

Put twelve pieces of paper, each one marked with a number from one to twelve, in a circle around you on the floor, with twelve o'clock straight ahead and six o'clock behind you, and so on. Or just imagine them to be there. Now make believe the clock is overhead.

Have a chair back at your left side to hold on to for support as you begin to swing your right leg, loosely and freely, up toward ten o'clock on the ceiling three or four times. ◊ Up and back, then up toward eleven, twelve, one, two, and so on all the way around to eight. ◊ At three you should swing your leg across in front first and then up toward three. ◊ Now change to put the chair on the other side of you and swing the other leg from two all the way around to eight o'clock.

If you have one leg a little shorter than the other continue to exercise with only the short leg (long one

161

standing on a book) until your legs seem of more equal length. It will take some time. *It's worth it!*

FEEL ANY DISCOMFORT AT ALL? GO BACK TO EASY EXERCISES!

The hip joint is more securely held together than the shoulder joint. You can build in a great deal of extra flexibility in the hip joint itself if you try to hold your back upright, head up, while doing this exercise. When you move as much as you can at the hip, your pelvis and back begin to move *with* the motion of your leg. They have to; the joint itself is reasonably tight. The pelvis and back give an extra flexibility to the whole area.

The farther you lean forward, the farther up in back you can bring your leg. The farther forward you can tip your pelvis, the farther up in front you can bring your leg!

But if you want to get the best possible amount of flexibility in the *hip joint,* keep the pelvis as fixed as possible! If you just want it to feel good and want *some* extra flexibility, let your pelvis go with the swing of your leg.

You *should* keep your head up! *Always!*

Your leg should *always* be straight! Point your toe half the time. Push your heel out hard the other half.

When you come up toward three with your right leg or with your left leg, sometimes point your toe up, sometimes lift the side of your foot.

GO BACK TO THE EASIER EXERCISE IF YOU FEEL TWINGES! HASTE MAKES (PAINFUL) WASTE!

Stand barefoot.

Put twelve papers, each one marked with a number from one to twelve, in a circle around you on the floor, like a clock, with twelve o'clock straight ahead of you and six o'clock directly behind you, and so on. Or just imagine them to be there—but overhead.

You want to swing your leg high on this one, after a while, so have a chair back at your left side to steady yourself with. Now comes the tricky part. Either make a bean bag filled with fishing weights that is long and thin enough to tie securely around your ankle (you only need one) or (I hate to say this) buy a weighted ankle strap from a sports supply store. If there are adjustable ones, great! Put the weight around the ankle of the leg that you're going to swing.

PLEASE BEGIN GENTLY. WITH ANY PAIN AT ALL, STOP!

Swing the right leg across in front of you and up toward ten o'clock. ◊ **Then toward eleven, twelve,**

**and so on all the way around until you're swinging
it back toward eight o'clock.** ◊ **Then put the chair
to the right side of you and work with the left leg
(again with the weight around the swinging leg)
from two o'clock around to four o'clock.**

If you pay close attention to your posture on these
movements, the first few times, it will become natural
to stand with your back up straight, head up high, and
all the swing coming from the hip, up through the waist,
but no higher!

If you have not managed to solve a short-leg problem
earlier, this version with the weight may bring some
hope. Try not to wear one elevated shoe unless there is
absolutely no way out. Quite often it will only make the
problem worse. Work as often as you can with this exercise and just see the difference it can make, with only
the short leg swinging. Leave the other one alone until
they seem even.

*For dancers and athletes, who need all the flex-
ibility they can achieve, this is a terrific exercise!*

If you're in good condition, start with a small weight,
say a half pound, and work your way up gradually. *But
don't use too much weight. You can get too flexible!
Guard your joints well!*

*Strengthen the surrounding muscles as you get more
flexible!* Pick some hip-joint strengthening exercises
from the "guide" to do with these!

Don't allow the added weight to swing loosely. Attach it
firmly to your ankle!

Lie flat out on your belly on the floor with your arms at your sides. ◊ Keep your head down throughout the exercise!

Lift your left leg straight up from the hip as high as possible and lower it to the floor again. ◊ And, of course, do the other leg. ◊ Keep your knees straight! ◊ When the exercise becomes easy, lift one leg up and down as often as possible. ◊ Lower it and do the other leg. ◊ When you can do the variations easily, lift one leg up and keep it up, and, bouncing as long as possible, lower it. ◊ Then do your other leg.

IF YOU HAVE BACK PROBLEMS, DON'T DO THIS ONE!

If you have a pot belly from pregnancy, beer, or any other reason, don't lie on your belly to do these back and bottom exercises. Look in the "guide." There are some fascinating variations there!

If you haven't been on your belly for a long time, ease things a little by putting a pillow under your hips, or wherever it makes you comfortable.

Lifting one leg at a time is an easy beginning for developing the bottom and some of the lower back muscles. *Really try* to get your leg up a little farther each time!

Keep your head down on this one!

If the area just above your bottom, in your spine, gives you any trouble at all, choose a variation of this exercise and work your way gently back to this one over a period of time.

IF YOU HAVE ANY PAIN AT ALL, DON'T DO THIS EXERCISE!

Lie flat out on your belly with your arms crossed under your head. ◊ Keep your head down all through the exercise!

Lift both legs up from the hip as far as possible and lower them carefully to the floor again. ◊ Try to keep your knees straight! ◊ A variation? ◊ Lift both legs and keep them up and bounce higher and higher. ◊ As long as possible.

NOT FOR BAD BACKS!

The bones, or vertebrae, in your back have different amounts and ways of movement according to the shape of the bone, the length and flexibility of the ligaments, the condition of the muscles, the way each bone is attached to the rest of the body, and the position the rest of the body is in. It sounds very complicated, doesn't it? It should. It is! But look how simple it is when you use it!

The spine is put together in such a way as to give your

back protection, strength, flexibility, and shock absorption—if you keep it in good condition! There is nothing quite so beautiful as a moving body in good condition. That's why watching sports, dancing, and people at work or play is so fascinating.

To be able to move beautifully yourself is a kind of pure, clean joy. The basic re-creation!

Lie flat out on your belly on the floor with your arms straight out in front of you. ◊ Keep your head down the whole time.

Lift both legs as high as possible and then lower them. ◊ Repeat as many times as possible. ◊ Keep your knees straight! ◊ Not hard enough? ◊ Lift both legs and keep them up high. ◊ Bounce them still higher. ◊ Really push it—keep it up!

NO PROBLEM BACKS ALLOWED TO DO THESE.

When you lift your leg, you are going to use a lot of muscles that work to hold your lower vertebrae (back bones) in place.

Because you are holding your head and arms down, the muscles toward your lower end where your legs are being raised will be working hardest. They will work properly only if you raise your leg *from the hip!*

Keep your leg straight! Don't bend your leg at the knee!

169

Now you're developing a nice strong bottom, back, and spine.

If you have a bad lower back, go back to the easy version or consult your doctor.

Aren't the rest of you beginning to feel lucky? You should! Take care of what you've got!

Be sure to do other back exercises to take care of bending, twisting, turning, and all other possible movements of the spine.

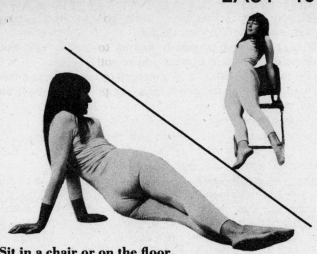

Sit in a chair or on the floor.

If you are in bad shape, you can sit in a chair, with your hands resting on the seat behind you, your bottom way out near the front edge of the chair. Make sure the chair is sturdy, that it won't slip.

Roll way over onto one hip and then lift your hips up into the air. ◇ Then come down and roll way over onto the other hip and lift your hips up into the air.

Or you can sit on the floor, hands behind you on the floor, leaning back.

Roll over onto one hip and try to lift your hips up off the floor. ◇ Then come down and roll way over onto the other hip and try to lift your hips up off the floor. ◇ Work until you can roll from side to side keeping your hips off the floor the whole time.

SHOULDERS OR HIPS NOT READY FOR THESE? JUST ROLL A LITTLE WAY—AFTER A HOT BATH!

You're really going after all the muscles down the side of the thigh, but along with them you're getting all the side muscles, the back and abdominal muscles, and the shoulder, arm, and hand muscles too.

All those added benefits! "Whole body" exercises are my favorites. *I hate wasting time!*

Start with the chair version and see how it's going to work out for you. If that turns out to be easy, try the floor version.

Don't worry if you have to start from a chair. It's the trying that strengthens the muscles. How good you already are has nothing to do with how much you are going to gain. Obviously, if you are weak now, you have more to gain from this exercise.

If you need arm exercises first to help you get to the point where you can hold your body up, that's no problem either, or not a great one. Go after your arms first if you need to. Because most people tend to walk a little at least, their legs will stay a little stronger than their arms. To keep your arms and shoulders strong, you should use them a lot more than most people generally do.

ARE YOU STIFF IN THE HIPS AND SHOULDERS? WATCH CAREFULLY FOR TWINGES! KNEES TOO! STOP! WAIT TO SEE WHAT TOMORROW BRINGS.

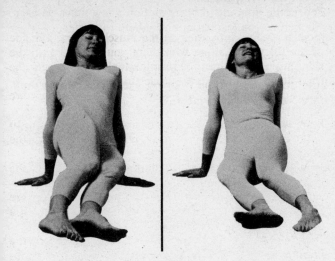

Sit on the floor. ◇ Lean back on your hands. ◇ Stretch your legs way out in front.

Lift your hips up off the floor. ◇ Start rolling from side to side to warm up. ◇ When you can, jump your feet from one side to the other without letting your hips come down to touch the floor!

DO THIS ONLY IF YOU'VE MOVED THROUGH THE EASY VERSION WITH NO PROBLEMS.

Besides all the good that you get from this exercise for the rest of your body, it is also quite good for those muscles and ligaments that hold your knees together.
When you first move into this exercise be sure that you just roll side to side a few times to ease everything up that you're going to be working with.
Then with your hips rolled to one side just jump lightly up off the floor while remaining on that side a few times. Then roll over to the other side and, again stay-

ing on that side, jump your feet gently up off the floor and down a few times.

Repeat the jumping in place motion a few times on each side before you leap from one side to the other.

At first you should hold your hips well up off the floor; when you have a little more practice, it's worthwhile putting a little more into it and letting your hips go a little down toward the floor on each bounce. *Keep all these moves under control!*

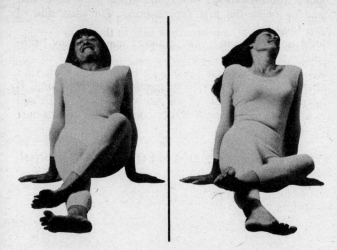

Sit on the floor. ◊ Lean back on your hands. ◊ Stretch your legs way out in front with one crossed lightly over the other around the ankle.

Lift your hips way up. ◊ Start rolling from side to side to warm up and to test. ◊ When you can, begin jumping with just the bottom foot turning with each jump from one side of it to the other. ◊ Then cross the other leg over and try it that way, being sure to warm up first, and to test. Don't try it more than once or twice the first day.

CAREFULLY! IF YOU FEEL ANYTHING OUT OF CONTROL, GO BACK AND WORK UP!

Talk about added benefits! Wait until you feel what this does for your inner thigh! Be careful that you get the feel of what it does for your inner thigh slowly, though. Start warming up by just rolling from side to side. When you're ready, begin the jumping with two feet side to side, and only then cross one foot lightly over the other leg and try very gently to jump one-footed from one side of the foot to the other side of the same foot. Just once or twice the first time around. On each side of each foot.

Build up *slowly* and you shouldn't run into any problems.

This exercise does give you a pretty good pull on your inner thigh, so *be sure* to *be gentle* in the beginning! If it feels uncomfortable at all, go back a step and build up a little more strength before coming back to this one. *It's worth it!*

THIS EXERCISE IS ONLY FOR A WELL-CONDITIONED BODY!

Go down onto all fours.

Use pillows, or whatever is necessary, to keep your knees comfortable.

Bring your right knee up to touch your right shoulder and back down to the floor. ◊ Then bring your left knee up to your left shoulder and back down to the floor. ◊ After this movement becomes easy, try doing it many times on one side. It's harder. ◊ Bring one knee up to your shoulder and down, time after time. ◊ Then do the other side. ◊ Make sure your knee gets as close to your shoulder as possible each time you raise it.

DO YOU HAVE PROBLEM KNEES, HIPS, OR SHOULDERS? GO TO SPECIAL EXERCISES, LISTED IN THE "GUIDE."

I certainly hope you don't have bad knees! This exercise is such a good one. If you do, see if you can find enough pillows, mats, or rugs to make it possible for you to do this exercise without any pain. Otherwise, don't do it.

If your arms are too weak to allow you to do it, take a few weeks to build them up and then come back. It's well worth it!

This exercise is mainly for the outside thigh muscles and the bottom. Don't feel badly if you can only get your knee up once the first time. All muscles in time respond to attention. Your muscles were meant to move and are healthier for moving. There are people who think that if you don't use your muscles, they disappear! They never do, of course—you've got them for a lifetime, and you *can* get them back into good condition with a combination of good food and exercise!

As with any lifetime guarantee, the care you take of the product has to do with the length of its life. Take care!

Drop down onto all fours. ◊ Bring your knee up to touch your shoulder.

Straighten your leg high up and forward to the side so you can see your foot out of the corner of your eye. ◊ Bend and lower and do the same thing with the other leg. ◊ To make it harder, try doing it many times with the same leg. ◊ Lift the right leg, straighten it, bend it, lower it, and do this again and again. ◊ Repeat movement, using the other leg.

ATTEMPT THIS ONLY IF YOU'VE SUCCESS-FULLY DONE THE EASIER VERSION.

If, when standing, you let your head hang forward, you will develop muscles in a hump on your shoulders to support the weight of your head.

In coming up onto two feet from all fours, human beings have developed a curve in the lower back from which the upper body curls more or less forward according to the person. The more forward curl there is, the more muscle is developed on the bottom. If we don't move the muscles that we developed as children, we are going to sag—and sag—and sag!

As you get up from this exercise, feel with your hand the way your back curves in just above your bottom. The more flexible you can get *this* curve, the better balanced your vertebrae will become, like building blocks, one on top of the other.

Human beings need some curve, and the stronger our bottom muscles are to support our forward motion, the more comfortably we will live.

Go down onto all fours.

Use anything necessary to get your knees comfortable.

Bring your right knee up to touch your right shoulder. ◊ Then straighten the leg high up and as far forward as you can. ◊ Now try to bounce it up higher, bend, and lower. ◊ Do the same thing to the other side. ◊ Need a harder one for later? Get one leg up and straightened and then, keeping it high, try to bounce it up higher. ◊ Time after time. ◊ When you recover, try it to the other side.

·DO THE MEDIUM VERSION FIRST.

I've never actually seen a leg drop off from this exercise, but it certainly is one of those that you'll always feel! Marvelous for that entire aching area you acquire from doing it.
It smooths out the large muscles of your bottom and thighs plus a lot of smaller ones.

Have you ever seen a four-legged animal with a sloppy bottom or thighs? Nobody wants to live on all fours, but there's a happy medium. Instead of chairs, always use the floor for sitting—and *without using your hands!* If you're too old for that kind of stuff, there are other exercises besides this one to keep your bottom in good shape. If you're used to sitting in chairs and don't want to stop using them, try at least to pull your legs up whenever you can.

Lie on your belly on the floor.

If you're just beginning and find the floor hurts your bones, try putting a pillow under your pelvis.

Turn the inside of your knees and your arches out and try to put your arches down on the floor. ◊ Only if your knees turn out too!

Push up with your arms until you can feel the pull in your thighs. ◊ If you don't feel any, try to put your feet a little farther apart. ◊ As time goes on try to get your feet farther and farther apart and your hands on the floor farther and farther back toward your waistline.

Make sure that your knees always are willing to turn out the same way your arches do. Go more slowly if it's necessary.

DO THIS ONLY IF YOUR KNEES TURN OUT TOO! IT'S NOT FOR BAD KNEES!

In a way this exercise is not terribly important unless you are trying, have been trying, or seriously mean to get to the point where you can do a split. In that case it can become terribly important.

You should *absolutely not* do this particular type of stretching unless you *also* do some exercises to strengthen the muscles very strongly through this area.

The stretching of the ligaments, which is what you're after, has to be understood. There are ligaments, very tough and very strong ones, that are wrapped around the hip joint to give it added strength. That strength is needed here to help hold the hip joint firmly in place.

If you want to loosen the hip joint a little in order to do a split, you must also strengthen the muscles that will help to hold your hip joint strongly in position. If you are very strongly muscled already, the muscle strengthening may be unnecessary. If you're only stiff, you need both. Test yourself on the muscle strengthening exercises (see the "guide") and find out if you are really strong enough.

Lie on your belly on the floor, on a mat or rug, with your legs apart. ◇ Turn your arches and the inside of your knees out to rest on the floor. ◇ Put your hands back near your waistline on the floor.

Push up the whole top part of your body to lift your pelvis off the floor. ◇ Bounce a little. ◇ See if you can get your hands back even a little farther.

The idea is to try to get enough stretch in your upper and inner leg so that you can finally bring your legs way apart, with the arches and knees turned out, and still get your pelvis down to touch the floor.
Nothing violent, ever, on inner-thigh stretching!

IF ANYTHING HURTS—KNEES, HIPS, SHOULDERS, BACK—ANYTHING, BUILD YOUR BODY UP IN OTHER DIRECTIONS FIRST! THIS IS A BONUS EXERCISE! IT IS NOT ABSOLUTELY NECESSARY.

Ligaments gain elasticity very slowly, but they all can be stretched, given time and patience. If you try to force it, you are more than likely going to hurt yourself. That not only doesn't help, it may also prevent you from ever getting to the point at which you can do a split.

A torn ligament can give you problems the rest of your life. Take it easy and the flexibility will come.

Not everyone will be able to gain the same amount of flexibility, since joints are built differently in each individual. If your bones will not allow you greater freedom of motion, that's it! Continuing to work on it as long as you're not violent is fine and will keep the ligaments flexible.

Very young children are in a better position. While their bones are still molding, if they are given the right exercises there is no reason why they should not be able to get to the point where they could do a split or almost any other move they might want to make.

I think *all* children should have acrobatic training! "As the twig is bent—"

Save split exercises for "dessert." Many others are more important.

Lie on your belly on the floor, on a good thick mat or rug. ◇ Have your legs as far apart as you can get them with the inside of your knees and your arches turned out to touch the floor. ◇ Place your hands on the floor at about your waistline. ◇ Lift your body off the floor so you're resting on the inside of your arches and your hands.

Be careful! Test first! Bounce a little!

Jump your feet up off the floor a little way, gently, keeping your knees and arches turned out.

Try to make the landing as gentle as possible. If you've had any muscle pulls in the inner-thigh area in the last year, stay with something easier for a while.

DON'T TAKE CHANCES! THIS IS A HARD AREA TO HEAL! IF YOU GET ANY TWINGES AT ALL, QUIT!

Make sure that the floor you're going to work on has no splinters or any other hazards that would lead you to make a wrong move. Best use a rug under you.

Test this exercise out by bouncing a few times first and then, when you feel reasonably sure of yourself, very gently try just a little bounce, bringing your feet up just slightly off the floor.

If all goes well, feel your way along until you can finally jump your feet far up off the floor, always landing with your feet turned out!

Always be sure that your *knees* are turned out! To do it with your knees in and feet out is going to throw your leg out of the proper lines.

Don't try to do too many the first day or days and don't push yourself to do so many that you tire. When you are freshly *warmed up* you should do such slightly complicated or tricky exercises. Don't do them when you're already tired from other exercises.

There's no doubt that different amounts of exercise make different people tired. The variation has to do with condition, general health, food, even weather or time of day. Judge for yourself—but judge well!

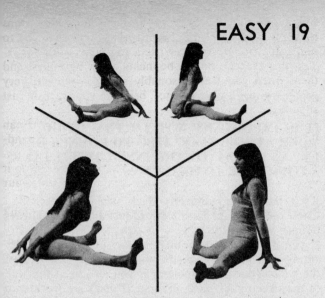

it on the floor with your legs apart. ◊ Put your
ands on the floor behind you. ◊ Roll back so
hat your back is very curved, as if you were
lumping. ◊ Then roll forward so that your back
very straight. ◊ Keep your knees flat.

Keep your hands or fingertips on the floor behind you
o help you keep your back straight. If you can't get it
traight, either *bring your legs closer together* or *put
our back flat against the wall* to do these exercises and
eep readjusting your bottom back to the wall each
ime it comes slightly away.

Bounce your upper body as far forward as pos-
ible, gently, with your chin up. ◊ Return to
traightened position. ◊ Using your hands for
upport, gently ease your bottom a little forward to
et more of a stretch on your inner thighs. ◊
Bounce forward gently again, chin and chest up.
'Lift your pelvis and chest up very high and
ounce gently forward.) ◊ Use your hands for

support again and ease your bottom a little more forward. ◊ **Continue bouncing and easing forward.**

Gently! Warm up first!

IT IS IMPORTANT NOT TO TRY TO DO TOO MUCH AT ONE TIME. ALSO TO BOUNCE GENTLY! AN INJURY TO THE INNER THIGH TAKES A LONG TIME TO HEAL!

Keep rechecking yourself: Back straight! Knees flat! Chest up! Chin up! Ease forward just a little and always bounce very gently!

If you don't seem to be making any progress at all try sitting with your legs apart but brace your feet against the wall. You have problems if you also need the wall to help keep your back straight. If that's so, work with your back against the wall until it is strong and after a few weeks turn around and put your feet against the wall.

Working against the wall is fun for another reason— you can actually see your progress! Try to get first your forehead to touch the wall, then your chin, then turn your hands backwards, put them on your knees, and try to touch your shoulders to the wall! If you can't get your knees flat, use folded towels beneath them until you can. Unfold the towels day by day and get rid of them as soon as possible. Then lean your hands gently on your knees.

ALWAYS STRETCH GENTLY!

Sit on the floor with your legs apart. ◊ Make sure
your back is very straight. ◊ Use your hands on
the floor behind you to lift and ease your bottom
slightly forward, often, to keep the inner thighs
stretching. ◊ Don't let your legs slip forward!

Lean way down over one leg to try to get your
chest to your leg. ◊ Then over to the other side.

Make sure that your knees stay flat.
You may find that as you lean toward one side, your
other hip will come up off the floor. To prevent this
from happening, as you turn toward one leg turn the
other foot and hip toward the back. Keep working on
this exercise until it is no effort to keep both hips down
and you can get your chest close to your leg and your
chin far out along your leg.

WARM UP FIRST! IF YOU HAVE EVER PULLED
A MUSCLE IN YOUR INNER THIGH BE SURE
TO WORK ESPECIALLY CAREFULLY AND
GENTLY!

If you make the swinging over from side to side rhythmical, the exercise becomes pure pleasure.

Take it at your own time and your own speed. Everyone has his own built-in rhythm. Some people naturally move and enjoy moving much faster than others. That natural rhythm becomes much slowed down when people don't feel well or if they are out of the habit of moving. When you first begin this exercise and are going for the stretch, take your time and bounce *gently* many times to either side. As you get your stretch after a few days or weeks or months, start moving quickly from side to side, stretching out and bouncing twice to one side and then swinging over and bouncing twice to the other side.

The warming-up period should never be left out when you're going to attempt this exercise. *The better the warm-up period the easier you're going to find it to stretch.*

If you try a hot bath before running to warm up, even if it does not improve your stretch much it will certainly do a lot toward preventing injuries. It is not absolutely necessary, but a hot bath before exercising helps to make you more flexible.

Each day a little further, not all at once!

Warm up well first with some sort of exercising that will get your blood circulating, such as running in place. Use the easier exercises in this series to get your thighs well loosened up.

Sit on the floor with your legs as far apart as possible. ◊ **Have your back very straight and the top of your pelvis tipped as far forward as you can.** ◊ **Put your fingers on the floor behind you and use them to ease your bottom forward on the floor as far as you can, keeping your feet in place.**

Turn one arch in to touch the floor. ◊ **Ease your bottom forward as far as you can and then lean over the other leg and stretch out as far as you can.** ◊ **Bounce a few times and try to ease the stretch.** ◊ **Sit up, ease yourself back, and turn the other arch in, ease as far forward as you can again, and again lean out over the other leg and stretch out as far as you can and bounce to ease the stretch.** ◊ **Each time you turn to the other**

side try to get a little closer to the floor with both hips and get your bottom a little farther forward.

KEEP EASING FORWARD, ALWAYS GENTLY.

Doesn't turning in that ankle make a big difference? It's really interesting how one little move can change things. This move will get you closer and closer to doing a split without being in a dangerous position.

Standing and letting your legs slide out into a split has always been a move to make carefully, even if you're young and in good condition. *It is absolutely necessary when doing a split in that way to have your hands on the floor on either side of you for support!* At least while you're learning. In this position, some people can't even get their legs far enough apart to get their hands down to the floor! (You're allowed to lean over!) With this exercise you can sneak up on the split, day after day, until one day you'll feel so comfortable with one leg straight out in one direction and the other out in the other direction that you'll know it's time to stand up and let your legs slide you out into a beautiful split. (Keep your hands on the floor just in case.) If you end up with an inch or two to go (with your hands supporting you), bounce gently and try to ease down. Then ease your back hip down to the floor.

NEVER STRETCH TOO FAST! NEVER PUSH IT TO THE POINT OF PAIN! YOU WANT TO STRETCH, NOT INJURE.

Do this exercise kneeling. ◇ **Hold on to a steady low table, or something like it.**

---

f you're just beginning, put a cushion on the floor under your knees.

Sit down on your heels and come back up to a kneeling position again.

Try to keep your back straight. Don't lean forward as you sit back on your heels or as you come up if you can help it. Use your hands on the table to support you as much as you need to. Hold on to a sink if you have to to *pull* yourself back up into the kneeling position.

Try to do without your hands as soon as you can. ◇ **When you are able to, come up pelvis first, leaning back a little from your hips.** ◇ **Put your hands out in front for balance.**

DO YOU HAVE A BAD BACK! DON'T DO IT!

The muscles in your high upper thigh in front are very hard to get to, either to stretch or to strengthen. This exercise does both. The ligaments through this area are also hard to get stretched out.

Especially the first few times, you are going to feel this exercise. It doesn't take long before it feels quite natural.

The exercise really does make a difference in how your upper thigh looks and feels. Dancers in particular need this sort of movement. In general, any body at all needs all possible movements.

This exercise will also stretch out your psoas muscle and your iliacus, muscles that are almost always strong in everyone. In fact, they are the muscles that help make your lower back hurt if you don't keep your abdominals strong. They also help you lift your legs as you walk, which is probably what keeps them so strong. They very seldom get a chance to stretch.

The movement will probably feel good to you.

Try it also with your knees a little apart.

ALL OF YOU WITH BAD LOWER BACKS—REPAIR THEM FIRST!

Get down on your knees on the floor. ◇ **Use a pillow if you need to.** ◇ **Sit back on your heels.** ◇ **Clasp your hands behind your head.**

Lifting your pelvis forward first, raise your bottom way up off your heels. ◇ **Try as hard as you can not to bring your head and shoulders forward any more than you really have to.** ◇ **Arch your pelvis far forward and sit back down onto your heels.**

NOT FOR BAD BACKS!

The muscles in this area, at the top of the thigh, must never be stretched *only*, for any long period of time. Especially here, you stand a good chance of weakening the natural strength of the pelvis. Choose some exercises from the "guide" to strengthen the area at the same time. Strengthening the area won't make you any less flexible. It will prevent you from stretching too far. A safety measure.

Don't ever do your stretching exercises without movement. Keep a steady slight bounce going on at least. With what is known so far, it is claimed that holding ligaments and other connective tissue in a stretched-out position for long *steady* periods of time will rob them of natural elasticity. For that reason *and* because it's fun to bounce, always keep at least a little bounce in the stretches or stretch gently but quickly.

Get down on your knees on the floor.

Use a mat if you need to.

Sit back on your heels. ◊ Raise your arms straight up overhead and clasp your hands.

Keep your head and your arms as far back as possible as you lift your pelvis up and forward as far as possible. ◊ Then sit back down on your heels. ◊ Keep your arms in place and do as many times as you can.

NOT FOR BAD BACKS!

If you can really arch your back, arms, and head in this exercise it's just that much better for you. Test it out first.

You could just go in for acrobatics, or dancing, or diving. There are lots of things to do that give you this sort of movement.

If you have a bad back this will almost certainly hurt it! Even if you've got a good back, don't try any twisting motions in this position until you've become quite strong with the straight up and down or forward and backward motion of the pelvis.

Make sure you're strong enough with the easier version before moving into this one. If you're not, you stand a good chance of forcing yourself to twist to come back down to your heels. With a back that's already weak, that's not exactly a good idea and you may end up by injuring yourself. *Take it easy!*

Keep your head up!

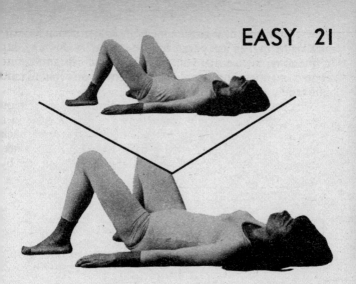

Lie on your back. ◇ **Knees bent.** ◇ **Feet on the floor.**

Blop your belly in and out.

No strain . . . Just let it go loose and push it up and down from inside. You can do this exercise from a chair!

This is just a simple beginning move to get your insides to wake up. Sometimes the muscles forget completely (or seem to) what their job is. It really takes very little to remind them and get them back to work again.

If you suffer from constipation or gas or have a large belly that hangs out in front of you, this is bound to be a good exercise for you. It's very likely that if you have any or all of these problems you are wearing a girdle. Do yourself a favor. *Get rid of it as soon as possible!* You could take a perfectly healthy person and put her into a girdle for ten years and almost guarantee that she would come out of it with a sagging, flabby, doughy belly. No one needs a girdle unless his or her abdominal muscles or tissues are paralyzed or separated (hernia). In fifteen minutes a day you could save yourself all that money and look and feel so much better you wouldn't believe it!

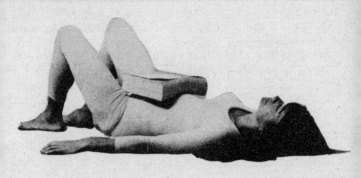

Lie on your back on the floor. ◊ **Bend your knees
and put your feet on the floor.** ◊ **Put a book on
your belly, or whatever seems to be the right
weight for you to lift.**

**Raise and lower your belly as much as you can—
as high and as low and as long as possible.** ◊
Breathe in to lift it up. ◊ **Close the back of your
throat to make a "kh" sound and breathe out to
lower it.**

Do you have breathing problems? That means you need
better abdominal muscles. This exercise helps to train
them to know what they're doing.

Anyone who lives a very quiet life has breathing problems. If you're singing, shouting, laughing, or even just
taking a daily walk, you will almost always have at least
reasonable abdominals.

You're never going to repair your body by wearing any
kind of a girdle or other support. The best it can do for
you is to fool you into thinking you're better. *But you're*

not! And you won't be until you, personally, do something about it!

If you begin to improve yourself before too much harm is done, the repair work takes a lot less time and effort. *Don't ever, though, think that you're a hopeless case! You never are! As long as you're breathing (even badly) there's hope!*

Increase the weight that you're lifting on your belly as often as you comfortably can.

Lie on your back on the floor. ◇ **Knees bent, feet on the floor.** ◇ **Start with a small child standing on your belly.** ◇ **Hold on to his hands (and try to keep him from leaping around).**

Raise and lower him with your belly muscles.

When you think you're capable, try someone heavier. *Preferably a friend! Never* use anyone you can't trust to stand very still.

NOT FOR YOU IF YOU'VE GOT A HERNIA!

You can carry this as far as you want. The belly muscles are amazingly strong when they've been strengthened.
Try letting the child jump around on your belly. Carefully! You'll be surprised. You can really do it! It's great for your belly. It has to be ready for *anything!*
Watch out for him when you're not expecting him to

leap on your belly, or always be half expecting it. That way you'll never entirely relax your belly muscles.

Another variation on this exercise is belly fighting. You need to have two willing people, yourself being one. With your hands clasped behind your backs, see which one can knock the other one off balance using only the belly muscles. It goes on in our family all the time. *Unbelievable!* (It's not easy if you don't have too much belly to begin with.)

If for any reason you can't work with people, try heavier weights when doing the lying-down exercise.

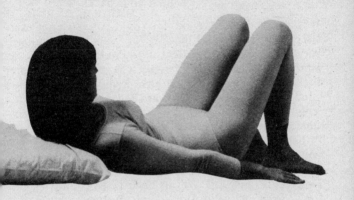

Lie on your back in bed or on the floor.

If you need to, when you begin this exercise, put a small pillow under your head.

Bend your knees. ◇ **Put your arms at your side.**

Now raise your head as far as possible and make a "kh" sound as you breathe out and let it down again, slowly, as you inhale.

Be sure to breathe steadily as you raise and lower your head. As soon as you can, do away with the pillow.

Raise your head and hold it as long as possible, but without holding your breath! ◇ **Then lower it slowly to the bed again.**

DO NOT DO THIS IF YOU HAVE A HERNIA!

The same day of a normal childbirth or a week after abdominal surgery this exercise would probably be allowed you.

ASK YOUR DOCTOR BEFORE YOU DO IT!

It is also good, very good, for you if you have not exercised your abdominal muscles for years and have been very inactive. It is excellent if you're bedridden, *if you have your doctor's permission!* It is great if you suffer breathing problems. If you have a very bad back it's a good beginning exercise toward recovery.

This would be a good exercise to do as often as possible if you're in a weak condition. There's no shame in being weak. Here is a way to build strength. And if you have trouble getting out of bed, this is one of the exercises you need.

Don't ever give up! We all have to live until we die. Let's do it actively! Don't quit! Just one more each day. Tomorrow you'll be stronger than today!

And the next day stronger—and the next stronger yet . . . Keep notes. See how many times you do it today, tomorrow, next week. You'll be pleased. So will I. Do it! I really would love to hear from you!

Lie on your back in your bed or on the floor.

No pillow.

Bend your knees.

Inhale, raise your head, hold it up as you exhale, and then get all the rest of the air out by making a "kh" sound and forcing all the remaining air out by tightening your abdominal muscles. ◊ **Then lower your head to the bed again.** ◊ **Take a few breaths and try it again.**

In time you should be able to do it more easily and time after time.

HERNIA? LOOK IN THE "GUIDE."

You're already a step further along! The next step toward freedom! Stick with this one until you can do it smoothly and with no effort. If you try to tighten up your abdominal muscles as hard as you can each time, you will really improve quickly. And don't just lift your head. Lift it up as far as you can. Make yourself do it *the best way possible!* Make sure when you make the "kh" sound that you close the back of your throat up as small as possible. The sound is like "cuh-H-H-H-H." Do it, tightening up your belly muscles, until you can't get any more air out. Not even a little bit!

If you have a breathing problem, relax and breathe a few times between each try. Relax and breathe a few times between each try if it bothers you in *any* way. (Dizziness, neck cramps, tired neck, anything.)

Don't push yourself. You don't need to. With consistency and time it's going to work!

Lie on your back in your bed or on the floor. ◇
Knees bent. ◇ Feet on the bed or floor.

No pillow!

Put your hands just under the edges of your bottom.

Inhale. ◇ Raise your head. ◇ Make a "kh"
sound and breathe out all the rest of the air in
your lungs by tightening your abdominal muscles.
◇ Raise one knee up toward your chest as you
inhale and exhale as you put your foot down. ◇
Then raise the other knee and put that foot down.
◇ Extend your feet a little farther each time while
still keeping the small of your back flat on the bed
or floor.

If breathing with the exercise seems too difficult, forget
it until you can do the exercise more easily.

211

When you are able, raise both knees together during the leg-raising part of the exercise.

NOT IF YOU HAVE A HERNIA!

Be sure your hands are only under the *edge* of your hips. Your waistline should still be on the bed.

If you're doing this exercise for the first time be sure to raise only one knee at a time.

This movement works the lower part of your belly muscles, while the head raising works the top part and the breathing tightens up everything in between.

Since the lower fibers of the abdominal muscles (the ones you can feel moving way down low in your belly when you lift your knee) tend to get very weak with lack of use, you want to be very sure not to work them too hard, too fast.

Lift just one knee at a time, until it is very easy to do. Then you can try it with both knees. You'll feel the difference.

When you can do quite a number of these lifts (take your time) you will be well on your way to improving a lot of problems—constipation, difficulty in breathing, sagging belly, bad back, improper posture.

It is sad but true that your self-confidence usually sags with your silhouette.

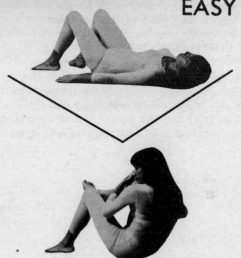

Lie on your back on your bed or the floor. ◇
Knees bent, feet on the bed or floor.

Breathe in as you come up and pull one knee up
to your chest with your hands. ◇ Breathe out,
making a "kh" sound, as you let it down. ◇
Breathe the same way as you pull the other knee
up to your chest and let it down. ◇ Keep that up
until you can: pull one knee up to your chin
(breathing in and raising your head at the same
time) and let it down as you breathe out. ◇ Pull
the other knee up to your chin and let it down,
breathing the same way.

NO HERNIA PATIENTS HERE!

Either you've had a nasty accident or you've let yourself
get into rotten shape. Either way, the important thing is
that you are trying to recover your lost abilities and
comfort. You'll probably make it, too, if you're consistent!

This is an easy beginning exercise for anyone who doesn't have a really bad back or extremely weak abdominals. They seldom go separately. Except in cases where an athlete has had a rather violent accident, you will almost always find bad backs and rotten abdominals on the same person.

It doesn't make any difference whether they hurt or not! If they are too weak to take a good hard day's work, sooner or later they are going to start complaining.

Do you complain a lot? Maybe you only need to move!

Lie on your back. ◊ **Arms at your sides.**

Breathe in. ◊ **At the same time that you pick up your head, breathe out with a "kh" sound and, grabbing your knees, bring them to your chin.** ◊ **Breathe in as you lower them.** ◊ **Breathe out and bring them up again.**

DO YOU HAVE A HERNIA? DON'T DO IT!

Your knees being bent keeps this one from being as wicked as it might be.

Every time that you shorten your abdominals when you're in this position it puts a little work on them. That's because you're using them to hold up your legs and your upper body. If you just lie there, you don't use those muscles at all!

This is a great way to start your day! Don't roll over to get out of bed! Use this move to get yourself up and out.

215

Even once every day would be 365 times a year more than none at all . . . and every little bit counts!

The pair of abdominal muscles that run right down the center are the ones that are worked most strongly here. Each is called *Rectus abdominis,* which means "straight abdominal." They are attached to the ribs at the upper end and to the pubic bone at the lower end. The shorter you can get these two muscles while pulling on them, the stronger they will become.

Without ever going on to a harder exercise, you could develop perfectly beautiful abdominal muscles doing only this exercise! *It's really true!*

THERE ARE NO STANDARD PRECAUTIONS EXCEPT FOR HERNIAS. IF IT HURTS—DON'T DO IT!

Lie stretched out on your back.

Inhale. ◊ Come up with your arms and your legs, exhaling at the same time, to balance on your bottom, while touching your hands to your ankles or feet. ◊ Inhale as you come down. ◊ Try it wearing shoes (or weights around your ankles)! ◊ Try it holding on to a couple of cans of solid food (or with weights in your hands). ◊ Try it with something weighting you down on both ends. ◊ Still going? Now increase the weights slightly.

THIS EXERCISE IS NOT FOR THOSE WITH HERNIAS!

This one should be tough enough for you!
And *good?* It not only works beautifully on your abdominals, but now that you're stretched out, it also works on your back.
It's a great exercise if you can do it at all!
When you first start up from the floor you are putting a

terrific amount of work on a lot of your back muscles. After you get up to a certain point you will feel the abdominal muscles take over the work load. Try to feel when the work shifts from the back muscles to the abdominals. It's fascinating how smoothly the body does jobs like this. Be sure to work your way up gradually with the weights. The first time around with *just a light pair of shoes* was wicked for me! I'd love to see some-one trying it with weights!

IF YOU MESS AROUND WITH HEAVY WEIGHTS BEFORE YOU'RE READY, YOUR BACK WILL, ALMOST CERTAINLY, LET YOU KNOW.

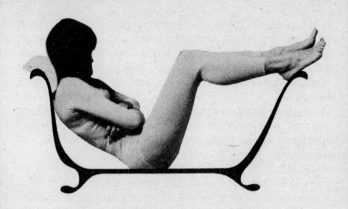

Sit in a tub of water as warm as you find comfortable.

Slide down into it so that your back is completely under water, neck too if you can. ◊ Put a folded washcloth behind your head for comfort if you need or want to. ◊ Put your feet up over the edge of the tub only if it does not make you strain to keep your head above water. If it's easier, just prop them up on the edge.

This is an easy flexibility exercise for bad backs, allowing the warm water to ease the spine into a better position.

If you need to, turn slightly to one side or the other to ease the pain. Use a folded towel *under* water if you need to, to relieve the pain. Push it behind your back or under a hip—maybe at the side of a leg to keep the knee from leaning out too far. Behind the shoulders? Anywhere *you* need it!

HAVE NON-SKID MATS BOTH INSIDE AND OUTSIDE THE TUB. THIS IS NO TIME TO TAKE CHANCES!

If it's possible, let a steady stream of quite warm water run into the tub to keep the water already there warm and also to keep a steady warm flow around the tub. Ease your back up a little every now and then to let the warmer water run under you, and to help your back loosen up.

If anything hurts, adjust yourself in the tub. Never keep yourself in a position that hurts. In this case pain is a special message from your body to take the strain off something.

Whatever it is in your back that hurts, it will almost always feel better if you can get it under water. The warm water loosens up the ligaments and eases some of the stiffness and discomfort, and the water itself takes a lot of the weight off the joints, easing the pain and pressure that way. If you've really got a very bad back, the tub (or a swimming pool) is the best place to do your early recovery exercises.

Don't let a bad back beat you!

BE CAREFUL BUT BE CONSISTENT!

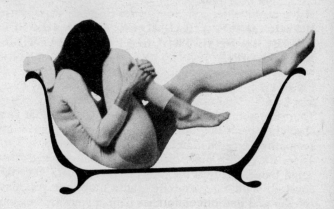

Sit in a tub of water as warm as you find comfortable. ◊ Slide way down with your back and neck under water. ◊ Lie there for a while until you feel your back beginning to relax. ◊ Be sure to have your feet draped over the edge of the tub or propped up on the edge.

This is good not only for your back but also for your circulation.

Now get yourself into a position so that you can brace one foot against the wall or the edge of the tub. ◊ Bring the other knee up to touch your chest. ◊ Use your arms to pull it up gently. ◊ Next brace the other foot. ◊ Do the same thing with the other knee.

Be sure to have a non-skid mat or even a towel in the tub so that you can, next, gently pull both knees up to your chest, if you can comfortably. *Have a non-skid mat or a towel outside the tub too,* for when you get out.

You're probably normal. Having a bad back tends to put you in a rotten mood. Attack your back (with exercises), not your family.

IF YOU HAVE A BAD BACK AND A HERNIA, YOU'RE IN REAL TROUBLE! GET THAT HERNIA MENDED!

I wish I had known about such exercises when my back was bad.

There are going to be times when you will feel that you absolutely can't take the time to do this. You have my sympathy. But sometimes there is just *no other way out!* There have been many people with backs so bad they could barely get into the tub, and worse, who have recovered. With care, exercise, and a little luck you may recover and never have another pain in your back again. Care simply means that you do not pick up or carry things the wrong way; test loads before you pick them up; never try to pick up a heavy load in a hurry; keep heavy loads close to your body while picking them up and while carrying them; and try to carry loads evenly balanced. But until you're free of pain completely and have been exercising or walking for a few months, you'll have to be extra careful even about how you turn your body in the bed.

Whatever you do, do not try to take anything at all down from overhead if you have a bad lower back! Climb up on a chair or something. *Lifting down can hurt!* Better yet—*let somebody else do it!*

Hopefully you will read these warnings after having been in the tub for a while. Warm water has a tranquillizing effect.

Sit in a tub of water as warm as you find comfortable.

You really have to have a non-skid mat in the tub for this exercise or you're likely to drown!

Slide way down for a while with your back and neck under water. ◊ Drape your feet over the edge of the tub or prop them up on the edge.

When you can feel that your back is relaxed, try this: Bring your knees up to your chest as you bring your chest off the back of the tub and up to your knees; lower both slowly. ◊ This should be one smooth in-and-out movement.

If you get good at this and it begins to feel easy, try a variation: Straighten your legs and clasp your hands behind your head, elbows forward. ◊ Keep elbows in that position as you bring your legs and your chest toward each other and then lower them slowly.

Then try staying up in a sitting position and touching your ankles and coming away time after time.

NOT FOR HERNIAS!

You're in pretty good shape if you can do these. *Take care!* At least put a towel under your bottom.

When you can touch your ankles easily, grab hold of them and balance. ◇ Grab hold of one ankle and let the other one loose. ◇ Repeat with the other ankle. ◇ Grab hold over the tops of your toes and straighten your knees.

(Bet I gotcha that time!) *Careful!*

Grab hold of the opposite ankle and balance. ◇ Then switch hands and ankles. ◇ Lean back and relax and just raise and lower your straightened legs to the tub and back up. ◇ Still leaning back? Raise both legs and, keeping one up, lower and raise the other one time after time. ◇ Even it up; do the other leg. ◇ And now to finish you up: Sit up again, keep both feet up on the edge of the tub, and lower and raise your lower back to and from the back of the tub.

NOT IF YOU'VE GOT A HERNIA!

A nice bath always makes you feel better.

Sit on the floor. ◇ Put your hands on the floor behind you for support. ◇ Bend your knees and bring your feet up off the floor.

Roll from one side of your hips all the way over onto the other side and back.

As soon as you feel you can, take your hands off the floor and put them out in front of you. Slowly increase the number of times you roll. *Be sure you roll as far over onto your hip as you can.*

NO HERNIAS!

If you're in really bad shape just *try* to get your feet off the floor as you roll. If you're trying, that's great! *You are building!* Don't worry about how unsteady you are at it. Think of the great advances you can make! This is a marvelous exercise for all the abdominal muscles. It's especially hard if you are carrying a lot of extra weight on your belly.

It would be good if you tried a changed diet at the same time. Diet means "habit of eating." If you are overweight your diet is wrong for you. It might be a very good diet for an active construction worker, but not for you. If you would rather move more than eat less, that's certainly better for you than sitting still and eating little. A beautiful belly happens to be a very comfortable thing to have. I don't think there is anything more horrible than to look down and see your belly hanging out in front of you—unless you're pregnant! You really don't have to put up with it! You can change it!

DO YOU HAVE A HERNIA? DON'T DO THIS EXERCISE! SORRY.

Sit on the floor. ◇ Have your hands on the floor behind you for support at first if you need to.

Pick your legs up and straighten them out as much as possible. ◇ Roll from one hip all the way over and up onto the other hip and back again. ◇ Now take your hands off the floor behind you and put them out in front of you. ◇ Roll from side to side. ◇ As your legs roll from side to side with your hips, let your arms go where they will to keep you balanced.

Try to increase the number of times you can do it each day. *A great exercise!*

NO HERNIAS ALLOWED! GO GET MENDED, QUICKLY!

This exercise is excellent. After *circulation* and *respiration* (how your blood moves and how you breathe) the strength of the abdominal muscles is of next greatest importance—or of connected importance. Both your circulation and your respiration are improved by good abdominals. This exercise gets all of the abdominal muscles in one (hopefully) smooth motion—three layers of muscle on each side and two muscles down the middle. That takes care of around three quarters of your waistline.

Your waistline is in good condition when it looks good at your waistline and above and below it.

Don't ever let anyone tell you that there is any perfect measure that you should try to reach. *You are unique. You are you and that is that!* Don't ever try to be like someone else. Do your best for yourself. Get yourself into the best possible condition and then be proud of what you are. Nothing changes your looks so fast as getting a firm waistline.

This is a comfortable and satisfying exercise to take on as a regular. If you need a daily routine of just a few exercises, this might be one of them.

Sit on the floor. ◇ Legs up in the air, knees straight (or almost). ◇ Put your arms out in front for balance.

Roll way up onto one hip and then over and way up onto the other. Don't just swing your legs.

For something harder, try these variations!

Pull your arms and legs up a little higher and keep rolling. ◇ Let your arms and legs down as low as possible, still keeping your waistline off the floor, and keep rolling. ◇ Put your clasped hands behind your head and keep rolling. ◇ Put your arms straight up by the sides of your ears and keep rolling. ◇ Bend your knees in very close to your body, clasp your hands behind your head, and keep rolling.

ABSOLUTELY NOT FOR HERNIAS!

Can you really do these? If you can, you're sure to already have pretty good belly muscles. These exercises are really good ones!

The abdominal muscles are rather strange. You will probably not be able to make them ache from overwork without an enormous amount of effort. There is something about them that seems to make them immune to the ordinary aches most muscles suffer from. Work away and enjoy your just rewards.

There is enough variety here to satisfy most people, but if you want more, look in the "guide." If you get tired of exercises, try scull racing or wrestling.

Here's another idea. Hold a weight in your clasped hands, behind your head, and wear weight shoes on your feet! Play around with them. They're a lot of fun with which to add refinements of torture!

Don't do too much at a time—save yourself for tomorrow.

ALL HERNIA PATIENTS TO GOOD DOCTORS, PLEASE!

Lie on your back. ◊ Knees pulled up, feet on the floor, arms overhead or at your sides.

Inhale as much as possible. ◊ Exhale as much as possible. ◊ Pull your belly way in and up under your rib cage as far as possible. ◊ Let it go.

If you get dizzy at all, stop immediately!

NOT FOR PEOPLE WITH HIGH BLOOD PRESSURE!

It you have high blood pressure this exercise may make you dizzy. If you do get dizzy doing this do not continue to do it until you see your doctor to check out the reason.

This exercise is to work on that muscle that helps hold your belly in. It's called *Transversus abdominus,* which means the abdominal muscle that "runs across" your abdomen. It is the third down in the triple layer of side abdominal muscles.

Other exercises will strengthen some abdominal muscles that *hold* the belly in; this set will strengthen the muscles that *pull* the belly in.

This is a good "bedtime" or "getting up" or both exercise. With practically no effort, just a changed habit, you can have a flat belly!

THIS ONE'S GOOD FOR HERNIAS! HOW ABOUT THAT!

Sit in a chair with your feet apart. ◇ **Put your hands backwards (elbows forward, thumbs and fingers spread) on your thighs just above your knees.**

Inhale as much as possible. ◇ **Exhale as much as possible.** ◇ **And pull your belly way in and up under your rib cage as far as possible.** ◇ **Hold it in for a few seconds and let it go.**

If you get dizzy, quit immediately! If you haven't got high blood pressure—try again. Each time you try it you'll become less dizzy.

HERNIAS STICK WITH THE LYING-DOWN VERSION!

This exercise uses one of the four muscles of the abdomen that help you when you laugh, cough, throw up, deliver babies, have a bowel movement, breathe very heavily, etc. It is very useful to have in good condition.

With this variation you are putting yourself at a slight disadvantage by sitting up. Lying down you had gravity working with you.

If you have a really sloppy belly it might be better for you to stick with the first, or easy, version until you either lose a little weight or make your muscles a little stronger. If you do try this one and when inhaling find that your belly still hangs out even though you feel as though you've pulled it in, don't worry. Just use your hand to push everything extra in to where the muscle is. After a while everything will go in together. Really! *Be sure to feel your belly each time to make sure everything is going in!*

If you feel slightly tired sometimes you'll find your belly won't go in so easily. Also if you've just eaten!! That's another reason why it's a good early morning exercise (before you get out of bed). Your belly is empty then and can go in a lot farther. Very good for the ego!

Stand with your legs apart. ◇ Bend your knees.

Lean your hands on your knees.

Inhale as much as you can.

Exhale as much as you can.

Pull your belly way in and up as far as possible under your rib cage!

Hold your breath as long as possible!

If you put your hands around your waist with the thumbs to the back and the fingers spread in front, you are covering a lot of the area and in almost the same way, minus the thumbs, as the "crosswise abdominals." Expressions such as "How does that grab you?" and "Pull yourself together!" should run through your mind. That really is what these muscles are for!
After you have done your inhaling and exhaling and

235

have pulled in and up as hard as you can, see if you can put your two fists into the cavity you have made. It's a lot easier if you haven't eaten for a few hours before you try it.

By now you should be getting pretty good at this. Try looking at a clock with a second hand and really see how long you hold it. Try holding it a little longer each day.

There are a lot of sheets of connective tissue holding the muscles in place. They are attached in different ways to the top of the pubic bone, the top of the hip bone, the line that runs down your middle, your lower six ribs, your lower back, and even up a little from there! Follow the lines of the attachments with your fingers. It's really amazing how much area they really cover!

If these exercises don't make you dizzy, go after them. You really can do an amazing amount of good for your innards . . . and your outers!

Sit on the floor with your legs out in front of you.

If this proves to be uncomfortable, try putting a folded towel under each knee.

Put your hands on your legs. ◇ Stretch up from your hips and bounce gently toward your ankles with your chin forward.

Unfold the towels day by day, until you can finally remove them completely. It will probably take a few weeks if you've been wearing heels (women and cowboys) or if you sit only in chairs.

If you can't sit on the floor or if you have a bad back, do this exercise sitting in a chair with your feet out as far as comfortable and slowly and carefully bend over to reach as close as possible to your toes.

If you get dizzy at all, stop!

Try to bounce gently down, a little farther each day. Stretching comes slowly—very slowly; take your time!

Flexibility is one of the ways in which your age is usually judged. It really has nothing to do with age. It has to do only with condition. We have all seen people in their eighties who are more flexible than others who are half their age or less.

You really never "lose" your flexibility, you only "misplace" it. It can always be recovered to some extent. However, maybe in a way it does have something to do with age. Certainly it makes you feel as though you're a hundred or more when you suddenly realize one day that you can't move as easily or in as many directions as you could a few years ago. It's your real age that makes *no* difference! Do you want to be flexible? You can be more flexible than you are!

Remember always to keep up a gentle bouncing movement when working for flexibility. *If you stretch and hold the position the connective tissue tends to stretch and stay stretched.* That's not what you're after. You want a body that's capable of doing many things. A body that's capable of bouncing back. When you want it to stretch it should be able to. When you don't want it to stretch it should be able to do that for you too. Bounce gently! Bounce Bounce Bounce.

Sit on the floor. ◇ Legs out in front of you, knees flat. ◇ Put your fingertips together.

Stretch way up from the waist with your arms over your head. ◇ Then bring your fingertips down over your toes (or as far as you can get them).

When you do begin to develop a stretch, try it this way:

Put your fingertips together; point your toes. ◇ Again stretch up from the waist. ◇ Keep your knees flat. ◇ Bring your fingertips down over your pointed toes.

This exercise will stretch you out not only through the backs of your legs but also all the way up through your back and shoulders. It feels especially good if you really pull *up from the waist* and forward, to stretch out over your toes.

Instead of putting your forehead on your knees, keep

your chin forward and try to get *your chin* down close to your knees!

Flexibility is terribly important. It is impossible in some cases to get your muscles built up in the right way, because your ligaments, tendons, and muscles are too stiff to allow you to hold your body in the proper position from which to work the muscles.

There are people who actually have beautifully developed muscles but bad posture. Quite often this problem can be solved with flexibility exercises.

It is best to test yourself out on all the different flexibility exercises before you begin to seriously build muscle! You can find them in the "guide."

This is a good stretch for bad backs!

IF YOU HAVE A BAD LOWER BACK DON'T EVER TRY TO TOUCH YOUR TOES FROM A STANDING POSITION OR WITH THE LEGS STRAIGHT OUT.

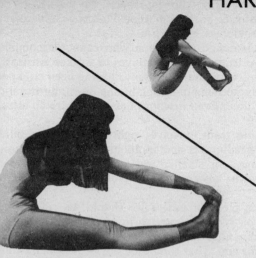

Sit on the floor. ◇ Put your legs straight out in
front of you. ◇ Bend your knees a little and reach
down and take hold of your big toes.

Straighten your legs out, one at a time if you have
to, and pull your heels gently up off the floor. (If
you can't reach your toes, start by holding on to
your ankles.) ◇ Bend your knees again. ◇
Reach over the tops of your toes with first one
hand and then the other. ◇ Keep your hands
there and straighten out your knees again, and
bounce your heels gently up off the floor. ◇ Bend
your knees again. ◇ Reach over farther, with your
toes in your palms if you can. ◇ Really stretch
far out from the shoulder with first one arm, and
then the other. ◇ Straighten your knees, one at
a time if necessary. ◇ Then pull your heels gently
up off the floor as you bounce.

Ease your way over gently; never bounce hard; never
stretch too much at a time!

This exercise will get you loosened up from one end to the other. Starting with your heels, the backs of your legs, your lower back, your shoulders, your upper back, your arms, elbows, and wrists.

I have yet to find the person who cannot accomplish this kind of stretch if he continues to work consistently. Stretching is a natural reaction to having been cramped in *any* way, to lying or sitting in one position for a long period of time. Even newborn babies will stretch after sleep.

We seem to train ourselves right out of this reaction with the headboards and footboards on our beds, our low ceilings, our smaller and smaller rooms, and our handed-down advice to our children that "it's not polite."

That's one piece of advice we should get rid of right now! If you yawn and stretch in someone's presence, it really means that you trust him enough to relax when you're with him. That should be obvious. Both yawning and stretching leave you totally unprotected. You would never stretch around someone you didn't trust, unless it was to show him that you really didn't think he could do you much damage. In that case, stretching would be an insult.

Compliment your friends. Yawn and stretch. Be trusting *and* healthy.

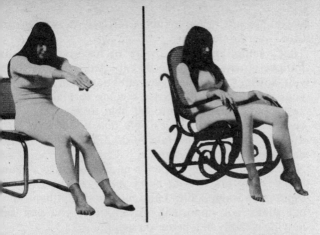

Sit in a chair. ◇ Keep your back just a little away from the chair back. ◇ Put your arms out in front. Keep them level.

Lean a little to the rear to touch your back to the chair back and then rock forward again.

Sit just far enough forward on your chair to make it difficult to pull yourself forward from the chair back. Don't jerk forward; make it a good, steady pull. Don't fall back; let yourself ease back slowly. If it's difficult to do slowly, sit a little farther back on the chair.

Breathe out as you go forward. ◇ Breathe in as you come back.

As it becomes easier, move farther forward on the chair, so that you have to lean back farther to touch your back to the back of the chair. Rocking is an even easier version. Never sit in a regular chair if you can help it. Either rock or get up and move!

NOT FOR HERNIAS!

If you are just beginning this exercise you may get very
tired—very quickly!

That's important to be aware of for several reasons
Fatigue is natural, it is to be expected, and it will slow
you down if you don't pay attention to it! If you get
yourself stiff or exhausted it's going to make you lose
hope. Only do enough to be able to feel that you've
been working—*even if it's only one run-through of a
exercise. It's not important* to do a lot today! You can
do twice as much tomorrow!

No matter what bad shape it's in, you do have a beautiful working body! *And every body responds to good
treatment!* Some bodies build more quickly than others
but that's not important. Given time, you can keep
moving steadily in a better direction.

*Don't let anything or anyone prevent you from being
consistent! Even if you begin with just one or two exercises, do them every single day!* Try to do a few more
of each exercise every day. After a few days or even
week or two, do your few exercises several times a day
That way you'll improve even faster!

*If you haven't exercised for a long time, don't push
yourself!* Start slowly—with few exercises. Results are
important—not time!

it in a chair. ◇ Keep your bottom way forward
on the edge. ◇ Fold your arms. ◇ Put your feet
on the floor wherever they're comfortable.

Lean back slowly to touch your back to the chair
back and slowly sit back up again.

Don't fall back to touch the chair back. Don't jerk to
get back up. Sit farther back in the chair, if you need
to make it a little easier. Or put your arms out in front.

To make it harder, put your hands behind your
head. ◇ Or lean back to barely touch your back
to the back of the chair and then just barely come
off it, time after time. ◇ Or do both the above at
the same time.

HERNIAS? FIND YOURSELF A DOCTOR BE-
FORE, NOT AFTER, THIS EXERCISE.

Some versions of this exercise can be practiced while
you're waiting in those thousands of different places

you have to wait nowadays. If you are exercising, you are no longer wasting the time. That alone might prevent some people from getting ulcers. All doctors and dentists—in fact, anyone with a waiting room—should have recommended exercises posted and rocking chairs available. No one who is interested in health should encourage sitting.

Just think how much fun it could be if all waiting rooms were turned into exercise rooms with rowing machines, treadmills, stationary bikes, door bars, and so forth. If doctors encouraged moving not just with talk but with example too, what a boon it would be to the whole country!

The best tranquillizer in the world is still exercise. You can prevent some adhesions with the right exercises. You can help a lot of back problems with the right exercises. You can benefit circulation with the right exercises. You can benefit respiration with the right exercises. You can promote the healing of broken bones with the right exercises.

The list could go on forever. Ask any doctor.

Sit in a straight chair.

If possible, use a chair that has a front rung on it.

Put your feet up on the rung or, if no rung, brace them against the two front legs of the chair. ◊ Have your arms out in front of you to begin.

Curl back, chin on your chest, to touch your back to the back of the chair and pull yourself back up to a sitting up straight position.

For a harder version, sit in a deep chair and do the exercise with your feet up on the edge of the seat.
If you get good enough at this exercise so that it doesn't feel so bad, try doing it with your hands clasped behind your head. Still easy? Put your arms up straight overhead, arms clamped tightly to your ears.

NOT IF YOU HAVE A HERNIA!

This is about the only good use to which you can put a straight chair. Sometimes I really believe that they were made to torture people. Have you ever seen the monstrous mistreatment our children get in school, sitting for hours every day in utterly miserable chairs, and on top of that, mostly told to keep still?

Children's joints, especially, are molded by their activities during their growing periods. It is almost as if we have set out to build physical cripples. If you ever tried to sit in one of those chairs for the hours that they do, day after day, you would never allow it to happen to them. And with the number of children in each class now, it really amounts to an assembly line of problems for the doctors. Worst of all it makes habits! Sitting still in school is a rotten health habit!

Wouldn't it be better to make the classes smaller and shorter? Not only would the kids get the personal attention that we used to get, but they would also get some hours to move in a world only half as crowded while the other children were having their classes.

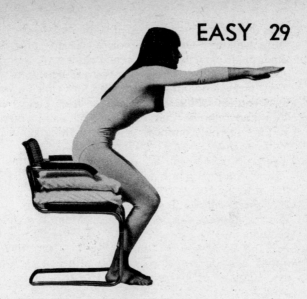

This exercise is done sitting down.

Pull up a sturdy wooden armchair. Turn it to face a strong table or low bureau. Throw a couple of cushions into it. Turn yourself around with your back to the chair.

Without using your hands, sit down in the chair. ◊ Move your bottom slightly forward on the chair seat. ◊ Put both of your feet slightly back. ◊ Put your arms out in front of you.

Lean forward and rise up out of the chair.

If you need to, use your arms to throw yourself forward! Use the table or bureau to keep yourself from going too far. Remove the pillows one by one as you become stronger.

I'm really sorry you need this exercise. As you become stronger would you write and let me know?

You should try to move a little more. Maybe a little more walking? Or maybe you could do some of the other chair exercises if you really can't walk well. Have you tried rocking? Sometimes you are better off with a cane, or even one of those contraptions called a walker, than you are sitting there letting go from bad to worse. You know that's what you're doing—and you know *you* are the only one who can do anything about it!

You *can* do it!

The arms of the chair are only to keep you in the chair in case you lose your balance. Make sure they're sturdy! We need you!

Use three pillows if you need to. This is for you in your condition—not someone else! Make it *possible* to get up!

A cane gives you a "three-legged" effect. Everyone knows how difficult it is to upset a three-legged table! *Make it easy on yourself—use a cane for walking if you need to!*

Now you should be standing. ◊ **But hold on to something extremely solid like a sink or a heavy bureau, at arm's length.**

Place your feet a little apart. ◊ **Bend your knees as far as possible.** ◊ **Keep your back and head up straight.** ◊ **Straighten your knees slowly until you're back in the standing position.**

As you get stronger, try to use your arms less and your thighs more, until finally you can do the exercise *without holding on at all*.

The femurs—the thigh bones—are the longest bones in the body. Looking at them on a skeleton you would think we were all knock-kneed. They slant distinctly in from the hip socket to the knee joint! Luckily the femurs are surrounded by many muscles, hiding the knock-kneed effect, which attach them securely both to the pelvis and to the lower leg. In good condition these muscles can raise and lower us from the ground and look smooth and beautiful! These muscles not in good condition become soft, flabby, and unattractive and let us down with a thud!

Look at the back of yourself in the mirror too! If you had been squatting or sitting on the ground all your life (at least when you needed to sit), that would be a *beautiful* reflection.

"Mirror, mirror, on the wall"! It's never too late! Give your chairs to a rival!

This exercise is a "natural."

Stand barefoot. ◇ **Throw a pillow on the floor behind you.** ◇ **Cross your feet.** ◇ **Lean slightly forward from your hips.**

Bend your knees and slowly sit down onto the floor.

Do not use your hands!

Rise up again by leaning slightly forward and balancing over your crossed feet as you rise.

When you can lower yourself gently each time, *get rid of the pillow!*

While you're still enthusiastic, sell the chairs! Buy some beautiful, warm carpeting with the money, or carry your own upholstered seat from exercising, which will allow you to sit on any floor. It's built in!

Do the medium version until it is easy before going on to this one.

Many of us really never bend our legs to lower our bottoms farther than the seat of a standard chair. If this includes you, you really will make your thighs and bottom horribly flabby! That includes men, women, *and* children!

To begin this exercise, go just a little way down and back up. Do it only a few times. Each day try to go a little farther down and back up.

Remember! *Posture counts in all movement!* Hold your back and head up straight and your chin level. The thighs should be strong enough at all times to raise and lower your body without assistance from your hands and arms. Can *your* thighs do this? If they can't now, they soon should be able to, if all you need is to make the muscles stronger.

If you have serious joint problems, it is not so easy a matter!

THOSE OF YOU WHO HAVE ARTHRITIS OR OTHER JOINT PROBLEMS, LOOK FOR FLEXIBILITY VARIATION IN THE "GUIDE."

Sit on the floor. ◇ **Your legs should be straight out in front of you.**

Use a folded towel under your knees if you really can't get your knees straight.

Put your hands on your thighs.

Breathe in and lean back a little. ◇ **Now breathe out with a "kh" sound and push down with your belly muscles as you lean slowly forward and slide your hands down along your legs.**

Bear down a little harder day by day, but never forget to keep breathing! Unfold the towel as your knees allow you to. *Don't ever hold your breath!*

This is a great exercise! If you are a very weak beginner, you can do this one! On the other hand, when you have strengthened your muscles and even become quite strong, you can still continue to develop with this. It is a very good and basic exercise!

If you're too weak to do even this one, or can't sit well on the floor or bed, try it from a chair. It is an important one to do. Just run your hands out beyond your knees as you exhale and bear down. Do the exercise without the attention to breathing first. Then add it on when you can. Don't be in a hurry! Take a few days or even weeks, if you must—the important thing is that you do it! And that you do it right! With just this one exercise, even if you're bedridden, you can have a much flatter belly.

ONLY PEOPLE WITH HERNIAS SHOULD RESIST THE TEMPTATION TO DO THIS EXERCISE!

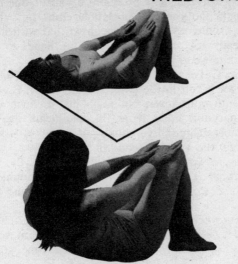

Lie on your back on the floor or bed.

Have something soft under you.

Bend your knees and keep your feet on the floor or bed. ◇ Put your hands on your thighs.

Breathe out with a "kh" sound and push down hard with your abdominal muscles as you raise your head and shoulders enough to slide your hands toward your knees. ◇ Breathe in as you relax back to the floor with your head and shoulders. ◇ As you get stronger, pull your feet closer and closer toward your bottom.

Why not try this one in bed every morning before you get up? Gives you a few extra minutes in bed and you can even feel virtuous about it!

NOT FOR YOU IF YOU HAVE A HERNIA!

This exercise may seem very easy on the first try! If it isn't easy for you, it is probably because your back is very weak. Do you have a double chin? If it really is difficult, fold a towel just enough so that with it under your head, you can then raise your head up to get your chin close to your chest.

Try this! Curve your hands a little, fingers stiff, as if you've got a ball in the palm of your hand. Push your fingers into your lower abdomen just an inch or two above the pubic bone. *Now,* lift your head! Feel those abdominals tighten? Everyone's got them! All you have to do is get them back in good shape!

As soon as you are strong enough, take the folded towel away. This will get rid of your double chin sooner and work your abdominal muscles just a little harder.

No need to keep poking yourself in the belly. That was just to let you know what is working. The muscles always feel absolutely amazing the first time you find them.

Only a few times the first day. You have lots of time!

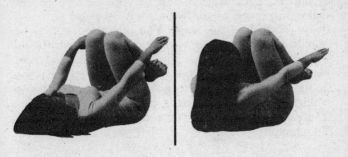

Lie down on your back. ◇ Your knees bent but with your feet off the floor or bed! ◇ Have your hands out in front by the sides of your knees. ◇ Keep your feet close to your bottom.

Breathe out with a "kh" sound and push down with your belly muscles as you bring your head and shoulders up. ◇ Then breathe in as you let your head and shoulders back down to the floor or bed. ◇ Keep your feet up!

THOSE OF YOU WITH HERNIAS DON'T KNOW WHAT YOU ARE MISSING! GO GET REPAIRED AND START GETTING BACK IN SHAPE RIGHT AWAY! START SLOWLY—WITH THE EASY VARIATION! ASK YOUR DOCTOR WHICH EXERCISES YOU CAN DO AFTER YOU HAVE MENDED!

This one is hard and can be harder! Be sure you work up slowly to this move! Keep your feet very close to your bottom, since this makes it harder! *Try to come up and down slowly with no jerking!*

Be sure to keep your breathing and bearing down sure and steady! If you grunt or snort, you're holding your breath! A rhythmical moan is all right.

Doing any exercise the wrong way is worse than not doing it at all, at this stage. You are far enough along now to know the rules! *Never, never hold your breath!*

To make it harder yet, clasp your hands behind your head, *but keep your elbows forward*. It is important in doing this variation *not* to hold the elbows back! You would then be getting at a different set of muscles. There are *other* exercises for those muscles.

Tough, huh?

Stand. ◊ **Put your back next to a wall, head and heels touching it.** ◊ **Tighten your bottom and bend your knees so that your back flattens against the wall.**

If you tilt your pelvis, hips, and bottom under hard to get your back flat, you are also using your abdominal muscles. *Tilt your hips and bottom under hard!*

Now straighten your knees and arch your back as much as possible and try to sit your bottom on the wall but with your head still touching the wall. ◊ **Move as smoothly as possible from one position to the other.** ◊ **Keep your head against the wall the whole time.** ◊ **Keep your heels against the wall the whole time.**

You can bend your knees a whole lot! It may even be necessary in order to get your back flat against the wall.

SORRY—THIS EXERCISE IS NOT FOR BAD BACKS!

If this feels completely impossible, go back for a while to easier exercises. You'll find them in the "guide."

If you have a curvature in your back that is just above your bottom, the kind that makes you look as if you have a big bottom, this is a great exercise for you. In some races this curve comes built in. Even if you have this built-in curve, flexibility will help you, which is what this exercise is for. If you let this kind of curve go too long, you usually end up not only with lower back problems, but also with a weak and flabby belly. Automatically this means that you will never be able to move comfortably again, never be able to breathe heavily without it being a great strain, never be able to have a comfortable bowel movement without taking a laxative, you'll get hernias more easily, etc.

There are an endless number of problems that come right along with poor posture. Something like fifteen minutes a day put in on posture and belly exercises can save you twelve to eighteen hours a day of little or even extreme miseries.

Do these exercises for abdominals and back for fifteen minutes a day for the rest of your life, and after the first three months you will never again have to buy a girdle, a laxative, or unfitted clothes. (Of course, your weight has to be right.)

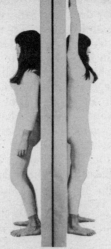

Stand with your back flat against a wall, head against the wall, heels against the wall. ◊ You can bend your knees as much as necessary.

Slowly ease your way up the wall but be sure that your lower back doesn't leave it for a moment. ◊ Try with time (weeks, months?) to get your calves to touch the wall with your back still flat. ◊ Pull your pelvis under very hard, and up in front. ◊ When you can hold that position, clasp your hands in front of you, raise them overhead, and try to bring them back to touch the wall, while still keeping your head, back, calves, and heels all against the wall! ◊ Stretch your arms up higher each day and back again to touch.

THIS EXERCISE SHOULD BE FINE FOR MANY BACK PROBLEMS. ASK YOUR DOCTOR!

Strangely enough your posture has a tendency to be related to your attitude or mood, as your attitude also has much to do with your posture. When people feel bad or put down they will almost always curl in on themselves, unless they decide to fight, when right away they take on an aggressive posture. Try to imagine looking very sad when trying to fight! Or standing very straight, head held high, while you're deathly ill. Or looking aggressive while someone tells you a funny story. You really telegraph to people how you feel by the way you stand, sit, and move and by the expressions on your face. *You can build both your body and your attitude at the same time because, believe it or not, you even telegraph messages to yourself.*

It is very difficult to look in the mirror at a flat-bellied, straight body with head held high and feel utterly *"Bleh!"* (Unless it's not *your* body.)

Stand with the small of your back tight to the wall, your head to the wall, heels against the wall, calves as close to the wall as possible.

Put your arms up high overhead. ◇ Stretch one arm up as high as possible. ◇ Then the other arm up as high as possible. Stretch that way a few times. ◇ Now clasp your hands up overhead and stretch up high. ◇ Bend from side to side just from the shoulders a few times. ◇ Bend from side to side from the waist a few times. ◇ Bend from side to side letting your hips go a few times.

Be sure to: Keep your back flat against the wall! Keep your head back against the wall! Keep your heels back against the wall! Try to keep your calves back against the wall! Keep your elbows straight! Keep your hands against the wall!

NO BAD BACKS!

Think about your spine for a moment as if the bone
were building blocks. If you stacked blocks one on top
of the other and expected them to remain standing, you
most likely would try to put each one straight above the
other, because you know from experience that that is
the way in which they are most likely to remain standing. If you then added other things that were going to
hang out from the front or the back, you would have
to make slight curves in the block tower to take care of
the added weight. And you know what happens if the
curves in the tower get *too* curved! *Everything comes
down!*

Our backs are a little better built than that, but not so
well built that we won't have to suffer the consequences
if we let those curves get too extreme. Our spines, or
building blocks, are arranged in a beautiful way, knit
and woven into a very pliable column by very strong
and elastic ligaments. That's why we can move as much
and as easily as we do.

But it's up to us to keep all that material in good condition. And it's the strangest material in the world. It almost always improves with use. We're always trying to
buy such a fabric! If you let it it will last you a lifetime
The miracle fabric!

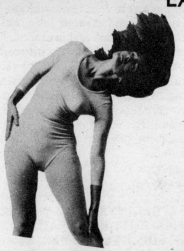

Stand in a good relaxed posture with your feet apart for balance. ◊ Keep your hips forward (swing them back and forward to be sure). ◊ Have your arms at your sides. ◊ Bend from your waistline. ◊ Slide your right arm down your right leg as far as possible, then slide your left arm down your left leg as far as possible. ◊ One slides up as the other slides down. ◊ Reach as far as you possibly can on each slide. ◊ Be sure to keep your hips forward!

BAD BACK? FEEL OUT THE EXERCISE SLOWLY, CAREFULLY!

This exercise should be excellent for you even if you're a complete beginner, unless your balance is bad. If it *is* bad, do the exercise sitting in an armchair and leaning over the arm to try to touch the floor. If you need to, you can even hold on to the other arm of the chair with *your* other arm, to help yourself along for a while. It's even a good exercise if you're the best athlete going.

The good you get from the exercise depends on how much effort you put into it. That is always what matters. But start slowly—you should! To be sure your hips are in the right position for this exercise, push them out in back first and then pull them forward, trying at the same time to tilt your pelvis up a little in the front. Keep them in that position during the exercise. As your arms slide, first to one side and then to the other, be sure your shoulders follow as far as possible. To make the exercise even better for you, inhale as you come up and exhale and bear down as you go down. Make it even and rhythmical.

If this is the only one you do of this set, that's fine! Just do it as well as you can!

IF YOU'RE A BEGINNER, BE WARNED! THIS EXERCISE CAN BOTHER A BAD BACK! TAKE IT EASY THE FIRST FEW TIMES, IN ANY CASE. ALWAYS FEEL OUT ANY NEW EXERCISE.

Stand in a good but relaxed posture with your feet apart for balance. ◇ Get your hips forward (always swing them back and then forward, to be sure they are forward). ◇ Clasp your hands behind your head.

Bend from your waistline to lean far to one side gently, then far to the other side gently. ◇ When you can, lean far to one side and bounce, and then come up and over to the other side and bounce.

Be sure to start slowly! Be sure to keep your hips forward!

BAD BACK? DON'T DO IT!

Putting your hands behind your head, as a variation of this exercise, forces you to put a little more effort into it. You also get a little more out of it!
People with bad backs who can do the first version easily will not necessarily be able to do this one with-

out acute discomfort! Try it the first time *very* gently
To do it right, you must begin gently anyway. In the
proper position lean far to one side and consciously
loosen the muscles down the stretched side as you
bounce quietly and gently—down-down-down, until you
really feel them all relax. Then do the same thing to the
other side. *Now* you're ready to begin!

Stay aware of those muscles! They must stretch as the
opposite side, toward which you're bending, tightens.

And keep the breathing pattern right! Up, inhale—
down, exhale and bear down!

Keep your elbows back and lean directly from side to
side!

tand in a good but relaxed posture with your feet
part for balance. ◇ Swing your hips first back
nd then forward into position. ◇ Bring your
rms up overhead with your elbows straight and
our hands clasped.

end from your waistline. ◇ Stretch your arms
ay over to one side gently; come up and stretch
ay over to the other side gently. ◇ When you
an, lean far over to one side and bounce; then
ome up and lean far over to the other side and
ounce.

eep your hips from shifting from side to side. Keep
our elbows straight. Keep your hips forward.
s you become stronger, add a little more weight at a
me to your hands. It makes a big difference—add it
owly!

**AD BACK? DON'T EVEN THINK ABOUT DOING
HIS!**

You really have to keep your arms right by the sides of your ears with your elbows straight for this move to be as good as it should be for your waistline! A lot harder that way, isn't it? And it can become harder yet. You must, though, work up to the harder versions, very gradually! Even you athletes!

To make it harder, start first with a *small* weight in your raised hands, and do the exercise that way! Build up slowly over the weeks to using heavier and heavier weights. The side abdominals are in three layers. Isn't it strange that the stronger they become the slimmer your waistline becomes? However, using the weight will, I believe, make the waistline stronger and thicker. Don't use weights if you want a skinny waist! These muscles are built to give you strength in stretching, twisting, and turning, plus a lot of other things, including making you a pleasure to watch move!

Again, the first time or two, loosen and bounce first to one side, then to the other. Make sure all those side muscles know what relax and stretch means!

Stand with your feet planted well apart for balance. ◊ Put your hands on your hips.

Bend way forward from the hips and try to stay as stretched out from the waist as possible as you circle your upper body all the way around. ◊ Be sure to lean well back as you circle back. ◊ Repeat the movement in the other direction.

NOT FOR BAD BACKS!

This kind of twisting, in any variation, is not for a bad lower back. It'll make a bad lower back worse!
On the other hand, it's marvelous for you if you have no back problems. It makes a good lower back better. If your condition is not too good, you might even try it from a chair (in a sitting position, of course).

Hold on to the arms and let your back arch backwards and then lean way over toward one side, roll way over forward and then up over the other side.

◇ **Roll forward again and on up to lean over the first side.** ◇ **As you can, let your arms get straighter and straighter as you roll around.**

If you are older and have spent a good (bad) deal of time sitting, and if you tend to get backaches, you really should be sure to ask your doctor which exercises would be best for you. Don't take chances! A bad lower back at any age is awful! *Really awful!*

If you're in pretty good condition this is a good beginning exercise to stretch and tone all the muscles around your waistline. Starting with your hands on your hips, just roll around gently a few times in each direction. After a few days, when it feels really comfortable, reach out farther with your upper body as you twist.

Stand with your feet planted well apart. ◊ **Clasp your hands behind your head.**

Start making small circles using only your upper body. ◊ **Continue to make the circles larger and larger, using your hips as you need to, going around and around, swinging down farther and farther, until you are swinging down and around as far as you can.** ◊ **Then come back up and do the same thing in the opposite direction.**

REPAIR BAD BACKS WELL BEFORE YOU DO THIS EXERCISE!

You'll feel a big difference in this move when you clasp your hands behind your head to do it.
This is one of those very good exercises in which you not only get at all the muscles around your waist but also test your balance.
Good balance, just like anything else, takes practice.
You've all probably been aware when getting up out of

bed after a sickness how strange moving can seem for a while. It can feel as though your feet are a mile away. Leaning over, you automatically grab for something to hang on to. It happens to older people too if they allow themselves to sit a lot. It would happen to you if you sat as long as you expect your older parents to sit. Then when they do get up and you see them staggering around, your first impulse is to say, "Sit down, Ma, I'll do it." As the old expression goes: "Don't do them any favors." It's a whole lot better to stagger around for your last ten or fifteen years than to die from sitting!

My husband's grandmother at age 103, when I last saw her, would not allow anyone to carry a chair for her. *That* is beautiful!

Stand with your feet planted well apart for balance. ◊ Grab hold of the thumb of one hand with the other hand. ◊ Lift your arms high overhead, elbows straight!

Start making small circles overhead with your hands and arms and join in with your upper body. Keep your arms tight against your ears! ◊ Make the circles a little larger and a little larger. ◊ Keep it up, and start using your hips to swing around in a large sweeping move. ◊ Be sure to repeat it in the other direction. ◊ To make it harder, start putting small weights in your hands, only after a good long while of doing it empty-handed.

Be sure to breathe evenly! Be sure to keep your elbows straight! Be sure to keep your elbows by your ears!

REALLY TOUGH ON BAD BACKS!

How hard do you want it to be? Always start the exercise without weights.

After a few weeks, when you can, do it smoothly with your arms straight up overhead—never forgetting to keep your elbows straight, never forgetting to breathe normally. If it bothers you—quit!

Hold a one-pound weight *securely* between your hands and stretch your arms up overhead. Do the exercise this way—slowly and carefully the first few times to test. As you want, increase the weights—*very slowly!* You will find that you automatically put your legs a little farther apart each time you stretch your arms out farther and each time you add weight to your hands. Most often your body knows how to make it easier for you.

If you ever find yourself holding your breath during any exercise except one in which you are pulling your belly in and holding your breath purposely, stop doing it! Use an easier exercise or an easier version of the same exercise.

STAY AWARE OF WHAT YOU'RE DOING!

Let's go after the easier, chair, version first. An armchair might be best if you're really weak.

Sit way back in a chair with your knees and feet far apart for balance. ◊ For beginners, keep your arms out to either side.

Lean way over to touch one hand to the floor close to the back of the chair. ◊ Keep your arms close to your sides as you swing forward with the upper part of your body, and over and a little up to the other side, so that the other hand touches the floor close to the back of the chair. ◊ Swing over and down and up, from side to side. ◊ As soon as you can, make it a smooth motion. ◊ Arch your back a little as you come up to the side. Now for the standing version: Stand with your feet far apart for balance.

With both arms down at your sides, lean far over to one side, keeping your back arched a little. ◊

Roll and curl forward and down with your upper body, coming back up on the other side to end in the same leaning to the side position, with your back a little arched.

IF YOU GET DIZZY OR YOUR BALANCE ISN'T GOOD, DON'T DO IT! IF YOU ARE JUST BEGINNING, HANG ON TO THE ARM OF THE CHAIR AND TEST IT FIRST. IF YOUR BACK IS BAD, DON'T DO IT!

What a waistline you're going to have!

These are some of the best exercises for flexibility and for the waistline. I've never really been able to believe how making all these muscles stronger can make your waistline smaller, but that's how it works! As they get stronger muscles also get thicker. Can they really be hanging so lax, so loose, that making them thicker and stronger can pull your waistline in? Yes they can!

Did you know that as you move, not only do the muscles grow stronger, but also the bones? Strange? Calcium, which is one of the components (or ingredients) of your bones, is laid down along the lines of stress as you work . . . maybe not right at the moment. But when your body receives the message "Look, I need a little stronger bone right here," it gets right to work laying it down. *If* you're eating enough calcium! Your body is also capable of making the *attachments* to the bones stronger! For just a little work, your body heaps rewards on you!

Stand with your feet far apart for balance, a little beyond your shoulders, since you'll be leaning farther out to the side. ◇ Clasp your hands behind your head.

Lean as far to the side as you can, keeping your back arched just a little. ◇ Now roll and curl your upper body forward and down in front and then up to the other side. ◇ End up in the beginning position, now leaning to the other side. ◇ Keep rolling over, down and back up, from side to side.

Don't do too many when you first begin. These, in the beginning, can make you stiff.

DON'T DO THEM IF YOU HAVE A BAD BACK!

Don't stand in your shoes or stocking feet on a slippery floor for this one. Once your feet get beyond your hips, it's not so easy to pull them in if they begin to slip. Sweaty feet will hold you more securely to the floor.

Your feet do need to be out farther than your hips for this exercise because you're going to be leaning far out to the side. If your feet are out pretty far, you can lean out more securely. The farther out you can lean, the more you can bend and the better you can work. The best way it can be done is the only way to do it!

Be sure each time you come up to the side that you lean back just a little and arch your back. It makes a big difference. Try it! You'll feel the difference.

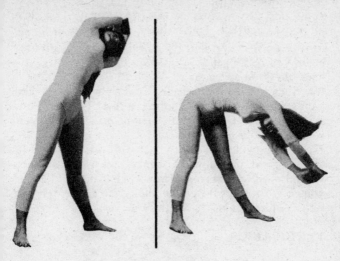

Now you come to the real workers!

Stand with your feet quite far apart for balance. ◊ Stretch your arms up straight overhead and clasp your hands. ◊ Arch your back a little.

Lean way over to one side. ◊ Roll and curl forward and down toward the floor, and continue to roll, coming up to the beginning position on the other side. ◊ Continue to roll down and forward and up to the other side in as smooth a motion as possible.

If you get really good at this and want to make it harder yet, try adding light weights to your hands. *Keep to light weights!* This will build up your abdominal muscles, side abdominals, and your back. All around your waistline!

NOT FOR BAD BACKS!

This exercise is effective, and you can tell that yourself the first time you do it.

Don't lean over too far the first time. Test it out. Slowly and gently. If it's okay, go right ahead, but *if it hurts in your back at all, quit!* By putting your arms up overhead, you really get to your lower back. If it hurts your back, don't do any more!

When and if you do decide to use weights in your hands, be sure to start with the test first! Try one! Slowly and gently! *Don't, please, try to do them fast with weights in your hands!*

The results will really show fast with this exercise. It's always good to know in inches and feet (the ones around your waist) just how well you've done. If you've got a lot to lose, you should be at the easy version. You're not ready for this one yet!

TAKE CARE!

Sit on a soft mat or rug. ◊ Legs out, knees bent a little in front of you, feet on the floor. ◊ Put your hands on the floor behind you.

Pick your bottom up as far as you can and lower it. ◊ If you are strong enough, or when you get strong enough, lift your bottom up far enough so that you can arch your back way up and your head way back, and then lower. ◊ When you are better yet, try coming up into an arch and then lower yourself almost, but not quite, to the floor. ◊ Then come back up again. ◊ Repeat that move without touching as often as you can. Save enough energy to get back to the floor without falling.

IF YOU TEND TO HAVE TROUBLE WITH YOUR SHOULDER, OR SHOULDERS, DON'T DO THIS ONE. REPAIR THEM FIRST. LOOK IN THE "GUIDE."

This exercise gets you several ways at a time. Not only does it do a good job on your shoulders but you also have the added advantage of all that work down your back.

If you're a beginner or just not in very good shape, remember, it's the trying that counts! *If you make the muscles struggle they are going to improve!*

And if you're really consistent, the part of your body that you're working on will begin to remember where and how it's supposed to be changing, and day by day it will remember better and better and more and more about what it is that it's supposed to be doing. In very little time you will have developed good habits. If you've ever made that move before, no matter how many years ago—two, ten, fifty, even more—it will be easier for you to do than if you had never done it before. Your muscles, your bones—*your body*—remember!

Easy or hard, if you're careful how you go about it, moving will improve your body no matter what your age. *No matter what your age!* You will feel like—you will be—a different person! *A new improved person!*

CAUTION—THIS EXERCISE IS NOT FOR BAD SHOULDERS!

Sit on the floor, on a soft mat or rug. ◊ Your legs out, knees bent a little, in front of you. ◊ Put your hands on the floor behind you.

Pick your bottom up as far as you can, supporting yourself well on your arms and one foot. ◊ Reach the other leg up and out to the side, stiff-kneed and pointy-toed, and foot turned out. ◊ Lower it back to the floor. ◊ Do the same to the other side.

After a few weeks, or when you feel comfortable doing the exercise, try this variation: Pick your bottom up as far as you can. ◊ Support yourself well on your arms and one foot and reach one leg up and out to the side and bounce it up-up-up, as long as you can. ◊ Do it to the other side.

DO THIS EXERCISE ONLY IF NOTHING HURTS!

"All-over" exercises are the ones that, in the long run, will do you the most good. They are difficult to begin with, especially if you have any "part" problems. Work on the parts until you have them pretty well leveled off and then start on the "all-overs."

You can get so much more done in a short time if you choose a few of the better exercises and put a regular amount of time in on them every day. Quite often in competitive sports you know there is a *chance* you may get hurt. In some games, you *know* you'll get hurt. *This* is not a competitive sport! There is no reason for you ever to hurt yourself doing these exercises.

If you are trying to improve only *your own body,* there is no reason *ever* to hurry or *ever* to take a chance. Take your time, get yourself over the worrisome problems first, and then go into "all-over" conditioning gently and consistently. Slowly and steadily you will find that each day you can do just a little more! *Be sure to do that little more!* Even training for a sport should be year-round training. Moving should be a habit. It is as necessary as eating and sleeping. Moving the right way should be a habit! It is as important to living the right way as eating the right way and sleeping the right way!

Sit on the floor, on a soft mat or rug. ◊ Your legs out in front of you, knees bent a little. ◊ Put your hands on the floor behind you.

Pick your bottom up. ◊ Kick one leg out to the side, foot turned out, and lower it. ◊ Do the same with the other. ◊ Straighten the knee and point the toe as the leg goes out. ◊ Kick one leg out to the side, and as it comes down start the other one up. ◊ Keep it up as long as you can. Make sure you're getting your knee straight and your toe pointed. ◊ For variety, try kicking your knees up toward you one after the other.

Don't let your bottom touch the floor!

WATCH OUT FOR SHOULDERS, BACKS, AND KNEES!

It's always a joy, once you've got your body moving, to see just what you can do. As with a car, you need to get your body started first, let it idle for a while, and then, after a breaking-in period, for a body that has not been moving for a while, you can build up speed. You must always be sure that your skills in handling improve as you, day by day, begin to build up speed. Otherwise you're likely to have a terrible accident.

With any car, the first few times out to drive, you learn little by little what quirks *your* machine has that make it a little different to handle from any other machine in the world. Anyone who cares for a car, a house, an animal, another person, or himself must find some way to work with or around the faults, some way to turn the faults to advantage, some way to make the faults virtues, or some way to change the faults.

Don't let anyone kid you—every machine, every thing, every body has faults. Those people who don't seem to have just learned how to live right. Use everything you've got, proudly, while working quietly to improve whatever else you can. On the other hand, there are people who use their public handling of their own disabilities to encourage other people. There are many "good" ways to live. Millions!

Sit on the floor, legs stretched out. ◇ Lean over onto one hip. ◇ Turning to that side, put your hands on the floor in front of your shoulders. ◇ Elbows straight.

Use both hands for support and both feet, as you lift your hip up into the air and let it down again. ◇ Do the exercise on the other side too.

This is another "all-over" exercise!

WATCH FOR PAINFUL SPOTS! DO SPOT EXERCISES INSTEAD UNTIL YOU'RE READY FOR THIS SERIES.

If this exercise is too hard for you, vary it slightly.

Sit with your knees bent, feet on the floor. ◇ Put your arms on the floor behind you and pick up your bottom and shift to one side to rest on one side of your bottom. ◇ Then pick up your hips again and shift to rest on the other side of your bottom. ◊ If your arms aren't strong enough to do even this much, do some exercises for the arms for a while instead.

There's one other version that might be easy for you. Sit in a chair, put your hands on the arms, and then try to lift and shift your bottom from side to side.

If you really *just cannot* lift yourself yet, do some arm exercises for a while and then come back to this one. It gets all the side abdominal and back muscles, plus the arms and the outer and inner thighs and the lower legs, feet, and ankles, and the shoulders, arms, and hands. You can do separate exercises for these areas alone, but this one is a time saver. If you're going to use it, you should also try some others that have you lying on your belly to work.

Try to shift the "all-over" exercises from easy to medium all at once.

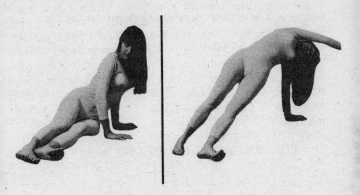

Sit on the right side of your bottom on the floor.
◊ Point your feet to that side, put your right hand
on the floor by your shoulders. ◊ Keep your elbow straight.

Putting pressure on your feet and your one hand,
lift your hips up as high into the air as you can
while stretching the free arm over your head and
out as far as possible. ◊ Come back down, swing
around onto the other hip, and do the same thing
to the other side.

Another "all-over" exercise!

ABSOLUTELY NOT FOR BAD BACKS!

Strengthening and stretching all at once make this one
of the pleasanter exercises to do. It also gives you some
balancing practice. Again it gets you "all over." Muscles all down the side and back and front come into action here.

Look back at the arm stretched over when you're all the way up and steady before you begin to lower yourself. Try to make your actions as smooth as possible. You may feel awkward at first doing any new exercise. It takes a little time for your body to learn just what you want of it. But don't worry. While you're learning you're using up a few extra calories and putting a few extra muscles to work. If you make a few wrong moves, that won't hurt either . . . We all learn from our mistakes, maybe even more than we learn by doing things right the very first time. Mistakes can be profitable! Just look at them the right way. *Don't let them discourage you!*

DO THIS EXERCISE ON A RUG!

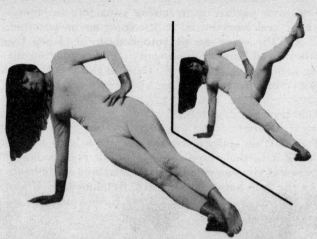

Sit on the right side of your bottom on the floor.
◊ Stretch your legs out to the right and put your
right hand on the floor down by your shoulder. ◊
Keep your elbow straight.

Lift your hips up off the floor as high as possible
by putting pressure on your feet and your hand on
the floor. ◊ Now, while holding yourself up, put
your free hand on your hip, unless you need to
wave it around for balance. ◊ Lift your upper
leg straight up as high as possible above the other
leg and lower it again. ◊ Keep raising it and
lowering it as often as you can. ◊ When that side
is tired, lower yourself. Swing around to the left
and do the same thing.

Try to do the exercise the same number of times on
each side. Try to build up the number of times that you
can do it on each side. Try to build up the speed with
which you do it. It's an "all-over."

NO BAD BACKS!

How about a few tricks?

Try, once you're up, to swing your free leg frontwards and backwards, as many times as possible. ◊ Do the same on the other side. ◊ Keep the other hand handy for support. ◊ Try moving the leg around in a circle. ◊ Then in the other direction. Shift to the other leg.

That takes good balance!

Try shifting quickly from doing it to one side to doing it to the other without losing your balance. ◊ See if you can do all these variations while keeping the free hand on your hip. Betcha can't! If you do manage, try it a little faster! Keep your hips up very high!

This series is great not only for your muscles and your balance, but also for your self-confidence—*if* you can do the exercises! Don't feel rotten—*practice!*

Stand facing a wall. ◊ **Put your feet apart for balance.** ◊ **Bend your knees a little and keep them bent for the entire exercise!** ◊ **Put your hands high up on the wall. Arch your back.** ◊ **Keep your head way up.** ◊ **Stick your bottom out.**

Bounce your back up and down gently.

With time, as you become stronger, move your hands slowly down the wall.
When you can, only barely rest your hands on the wall.
Try to get your back parallel to the floor when you're strong enough.

THIS IS NOT FOR BAD BACKS!

If for any reason you can't lie on your belly on the floor (sometimes it's because of a big belly, bad knees, stiffness that does not allow you to roll over, maybe even the fact that you just happened to get dressed first), you can use this series to begin getting your back into good shape. *But not if you have a bad back!*

Always start with your back not too far arched in case of any weakness. That is also why you should start with your hands *on* the wall. The wall gives you a lot of extra support while you get "the feel" of your back. Especially when you're just beginning, it is important to do only the straight up and down movements.

If you don't know what to look for in the form of trouble, watch for slight "catches" or small sharp pains. If it is just catches, work with your hands high up on the wall for a while until there are no catches. If there is any pain at all, do for a long time lots of exercises for the abdominals and for back flexibility, then try again. Check your knees! *Keep them bent!*

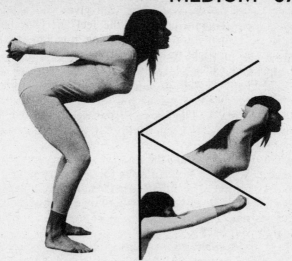

Stand with your feet apart for balance. ◇ **Stick your bottom out.** ◇ **Bend your knees slightly.** ◇ **Arch your back.** ◇ **Keep your head up.** ◇ **Bend from the hips straight forward, head still up.** ◇ **Clasp your hands behind your back.**

Bounce gently up and down, being sure to keep your head up, knees bent, and back arched.

If your back "rounds" over, you're not doing it right. Arch it! Now try it with your hands clasped behind your head! Only if you can keep your back arched!
Don't be embarrassed to go back to an easier step. It's important to do it right and, anyway, you'll soon catch up.
If you can keep your arms level with your chin, try it next with your arms held out in front. If your arms sink or your back "rounds," go back a step. Your knees are bound to get tired in this position. Straighten up every

now and then to give them a rest. In time you'll get stronger.

NOT FOR BAD BACKS!

These can be pretty tough when you first begin them. Really, *don't* do too many to begin with! Letting your weight "hang out" from your hips this way is work! It will quickly become easy if you are sure to take it one step at a time and make each step right. Don't, under any circumstances, keep working if you get a catch in your back.

If you do, sit down on the floor and roll up into a ball, or sit down, grab hold of your toes, and try to stretch your knees out straight. It doesn't make any difference whether you can or not, only that you stretch your back muscles out. You are working those muscles that serve to arch your back.

There are so many connections along your rib cage and your spinal column to the skull and to connective tissue that attaches to the pelvis. The whole thing looks very neat, but it's really sort of unbelievably complicated. You just have to recognize that if you had the bones of a human skeleton and had to connect them all together in the best possible way to do the jobs they have to do, you'd have no choice but to do it the way it's done. Keep checking! Are your knees bent?

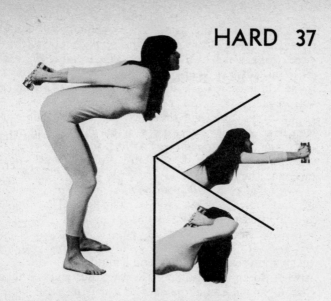

Stand with your feet apart for balance. ◇ Stick your bottom out. ◇ Bend your knees slightly. ◇ Arch your back. ◇ Keep your head up. ◇ Bend from the hips to come straight forward—head still up. ◇ Now you must keep your position exactly as above.

Start with a small weight in your hands. ◇ Bounce gently with your hands clasped behind your back, still holding the weight. ◇ Bounce gently with your hands clasped behind your head, still holding the weight. ◇ Bounce gently with your arms out in front of you at chin level, still holding the weight.

Take your time! Don't increase the weight too rapidly! If you feel any discomfort in your back at all, quit immediately! Do the motion more gently, with less weight!

You can really develop with this series, but don't forget that you need to use, with these, the back exercises that move you from side to side. The abdominals should always be made strong first! *Until your abdominals are very strong you would be better off not doing these at all!* You can give yourself a rotten, even injured, back by developing the back muscles and leaving the front of you weak.

If, once you do begin these, you find that when you lean over *you bend forward very abruptly at the neck and your arms drop down in front,* forget these exercises for a while and do some for the upper back, posture, and shoulders.

If you bend over with your shoulders hunched, do the back exercises that have you on your belly. They'll give you more support—and don't, for a while, do those with your arms out in front of you.

If you bend halfway in between these two areas, do, instead, those exercises for round shoulders.

Always do an exercise the right way; thus you can take care of an enormous number of small physical problems. *Look for trouble,* so you can repair it!

Get on your hands and knees on the floor (on a mat).

Push up with your knees until you're resting only on your hands and feet. ◊ **Come down again gently.**

IF ANYTHING HURTS, STOP!

You may find that if you put your hands a little farther forward it will be easier to raise your knees up off the floor. It also helps to put your knees and feet a little farther apart.

If your arms aren't anywhere near strong enough to do this, look in the "guide" for the standing shoulder exercises and work your way along to this. It takes some time, but we've all got the rest of our lives.

For a reassuring beginning you could try raising just one knee off the floor at a time. Lower one before raising the other. When you feel brave enough and strong enough, try raising one, keep it up, and raise the other one also. If it's easier you could lower them the same way, one at a time. Be very careful, however you decide to do it.

Keep a soft mat under your knees! *The best way is the safe way. Take your time!*

Stand with your feet a little apart. ◇ Lean over to put your hands on the floor, and keep them about twelve or fifteen inches apart in line with your shoulders for good balance.

Walk out with your hands until you're lying flat out on your belly. ◇ Now walk up with your feet until you're back in the original position.

If you're ready for this one you are also ready to *hold your belly in while you do it!*

As soon as you feel sure enough of yourself start keeping your hands closer together and your feet closer together. As if there were a straight line drawn along the floor and you were trying to walk it with your hands and feet.

DON'T TRY THIS UNTIL THE EASY VERSION IS EASY!

This is a pretty good exercise. It gets your arms, shoulders, hands, back, belly, hamstrings, and feet, and it's good for balance, too! It's an "all-over."

Any exercise that has you on all fours, either back down or belly down, with an unsupported middle is going to do you a lot of good all over. All fours meaning hands and feet rather than hands and knees. If you don't have time for a lot of exercises, choose a few that get you "all over" and stick with them. *Do your whole body all at once!*

Be sure that you can do quite a few of these before you go on to the next, harder, version. You need to be in pretty good condition to move into the "all-over" exercises. Otherwise you're likely to injure some weak part. Make sure that you work sensibly. Work up your weak parts *first* and then go on to the more complete exercises, such as this one. Two or three "all-over" exercises can take the place of six or eight "separate" exercises. That's a real time saver!

Stand with your feet a little apart. ◇ Lean over to put your hands on the floor, or just come down into a squat.

Jump your feet back to get your legs out as straight as possible behind you. ◇ Then jump them up into a squat position. ◇ Continue to jump them in and out.

DON'T TRY THIS BEFORE WORKING THROUGH EASY AND MEDIUM VERSIONS.

This one is a little harder. You have to "brake" the downward thrust of your body to keep from landing belly first on the floor. That means you'll be tightening your back and belly muscles very quickly to make them rigid enough to hold you above ground level.

The exercise won't be nearly good enough if you don't get your legs out reasonably straight. When you first begin it's all right to do it only partially if just to get the feel of it, but as soon as you can, start working to get those legs out straight.

You should always work to do each exercise with as much "class" as possible. Exercises done correctly usually look fabulous! You get *more* benefit from any movement that's done *correctly*.

If your legs don't go back far enough your midsection is not going to have to work half as hard and so it will not *get* half as hard! This exercise is going to work your midsection and your legs much harder than it will your shoulders. They won't be neglected, though. More later.

If this movement gets easy, work faster and with the legs straighter.

An "all-over" exercise!

Lie on your belly on the floor. ◊ Tuck your toes under to put their bottom sides on the floor. ◊ Lay your forearms (from elbow to hand) on the floor, hands in front of you.

Putting pressure on your forearms and your toes, lift your middle up off the floor.

If you're just beginning it's okay to pick your middle way up. If you're strong enough, just lift your body until it makes a straight line and then lower it to the floor again. Try, when you can, to lift it time after time.

DON'T DO THIS EXERCISE IF IT HURTS ANY-WHERE.

If you find it impossible to lie on your belly, look in the "guide." There's another version, for beginning push-ups. If this one is very hard for you, remember that even *trying* is going to work a lot of muscles! Again, that easier version is a good one to try.

You have altogether 434 voluntary muscles and it *feels* as though you're using just about all of them in this exercise! One try is plenty for a beginning! This exercise deserves a place with the "all-overs," even though the arms aren't getting a whole lot of activity. Add an extra, and moving, arm exercise if you're going to do this one. It really pays off to look yourself over well and choose those moves that will most benefit *you!* If you can develop ways of living that will take care of your weak spots, that's the best way. Otherwise choose those exercises you need most and do them.

Lie on your belly on the floor. ◇ Tuck your toes under to put their bottom sides on the floor. ◇ Put your forearms (from elbow to hand) on the floor.

Putting pressure on your forearms and your toes, lift your middle up off the floor. ◇ Hold your middle up while you lift first one leg and then the other up as high as possible off the floor while keeping your back level. ◇ Lift your legs from the hip! Don't let your bottom stick up in the air!

CAREFULLY! DON'T DO IT IF IT HURTS!

Every human activity is good in the eyes of "The Great Body Builder," though maybe not always the motives behind them.

A moving body is renewing-rebuilding itself. Your body constantly adjusts to just those things you ask of it. If you ask only that it lift you from your bed to your chair, that it carry you only from your seat at the table to your seat in the car, or from the table to the television, it will never be able to do much more than that without real stress or discomfort. Weekend workouts are really not treating it fairly, as dozens, hundreds, thousands of men with heart attacks can tell you. *Those who still can!*

I've often wondered whether the reason, or at least one of them, that women have fewer heart attacks is because traditionally they always do the housework. When I realized that my husband was not going to go to the YMCA any more I decided that the least I could do for him was not to put his laundry away for him. Every morning he has to go down to the basement for his clean clothes. That's not a dirty trick—that's a clean trick!

Lie on your belly on the floor. ◇ Tuck your toes under to put their bottom sides on the floor. ◇ Put your forearms (from elbow to hand) on the floor.

Putting pressure on your forearms and your toes, lift your middle up off the floor. ◇ Hold your middle up level with the floor while you rest your weight on one foot, raise the other leg from the hip, out a little to the side, and bounce it up, up, up as many times as possible. ◇ Come down, and then go up again with the other side, or just stay up if you can and shift to do it to the other side.

See how many times you can do it on one side before shifting to the other. Start on your weaker side.

BE SURE TO WORK THROUGH EASIER VERSIONS FIRST!

This one gets to everyone! It is great for the whole body and especially good for the outside of your thighs and your bottom.

For a slight variation you could try, just for fun, coming down and up, extending one leg and lowering it, and then down and up and extending the other leg out and lowering it. This variation keeps you adjusting your weight a little more constantly. The more movement and adjustment involved, the better. Murder!

There isn't anything much to watch out for. You can't easily do too many of these. They're too tough and have you in too difficult a position to hold for too long. Men will find it easier to do than women, since they have more muscle built in to begin with. Women will find it more important to do than men since they have the hip problems. At least a lot more often than men.

You men with hip problems—change quickly! Women watch men's bottoms too. It's perfectly natural. Moving bodies do attract attention—and muscles are beautiful. Don't sag along! Muscles should be elastic!

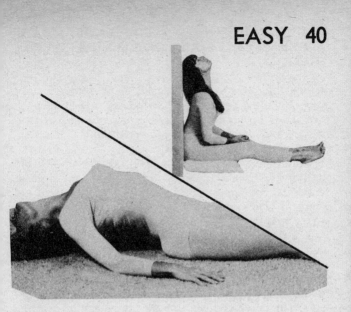

Sit on the floor.

Try this exercise first against the wall. If you can't get your knees flat on the floor put a cushion under your bottom or under your knees, whichever makes you feel most comfortable.

Sit with your bottom flat and back tightly against the wall.

Arch your back as hard as you can and try to bring the top of your head to touch the wall. ◊ **Relax to flatten your back to the wall again.** ◊ **When you can, try it from a lying-down position: flat on your back on a cushion or mat.** ◊ **Use your arms by your sides, if necessary, to arch your back up by sliding your head under, until you're arched up from your bottom to the top of your head.** ◊ **Ease yourself down again.**

NOT IF YOU'VE GOT A WHIPLASH OR ANY OTHER NECK PROBLEMS! DANGER! ATTENTION!

Before doing this exercise, please, go back to yet easier exercises in the "guide" and work your way up through them first. *Be forewarned! This series can hurt if your neck or your back is not in good condition!* If that's so, look for easier back exercises!

Be sure when you first begin to do this exercise from the floor to have your hands and arms on the floor at your sides to support you until you know that it is not going to give you any trouble. Go into the arch very slowly and carefully, and if you need to help yourself into or down out of the arch, use a *lot* of support from your arms.

There are so many small muscles all along the spine to strengthen the neck, both to the outside to arch it and to the belly to curl it—you would find it hard to believe. The curve you get with this move is mostly in the lower back and a little above it. There is also a slight curve you get in the neck and just a little way below it.

IF YOU HAVE PROBLEMS WITH EITHER YOUR NECK OR A BAD LOWER BACK, DON'T DO THIS ONE.

Lie on your back on the floor. ◇ Pull your knees
up, feet flat on the floor. ◇ Put your hands backwards, palms down, by your ears.

Push up with your bottom until you're resting on
the top of your head, your hands, and your feet. ◇
Come down again, carefully.

After a few weeks, when you're more sure of yourself,
try these variations.

Resting on the top of your head and your feet,
raise your arms up and overhead to touch the floor
behind you. ◇ Or, resting on the top of your head
and your feet, take your hands off the floor and
rock, very little and very gently, back and forth
between your head and your feet. ◇ Or, try to get
your feet a little closer each day. Move them in
closer to your bottom before you lift off, or move
your head in a little toward your feet, using your
hands for support as you rearrange yourself.

317

Always support your head and neck well with your hands until you feel no uncertainty at all about whether you can do it with your head and neck alone.

NOT FOR BAD BACKS OR NECKS!

The only things that might prevent you from doing this exercise are the unusual position and the terror of the unknown. Don't be afraid to try it. If you try it for several days in a row, all of a sudden it's no longer a strange position. Everyone starts off saying, "Oh, I couldn't do that!" A few days later comes a voice, "I did it! I did it!" If only because it makes you feel so accomplished, you should try it.

All the back muscles being used in this move are attached to the spinal column toward the outside. Put your fingers on either side of your spinal column (not while you're upside down, please) in your lower back, where most of the movement happens with this exercise, and arch your back in as far as you can. Really, as far as you can! Feel the muscles move? That (I only just noticed, myself) is the move that people automatically make when they've been sitting slumped for long periods of time. Slumping keeps these muscles stretched. To pull them up tight as in this movement gives a certain amount of relief. That should make this exercise a good one for office workers.

Of course, if you're doing office work, you could just straighten up hard in your chair, every now and then.

Lie on your back on the floor. ◇ **Pull your knees up, feet flat on the floor.** ◇ **Put your hands backwards, palms down, on the floor.**

Pushing up, first with your bottom and then with your head, put all your weight on your feet and your hands. ◇ **Arch up as high as you can, always remembering to keep enough strength to get you down safely!**

Try to look back at your feet, or at least the floor. When you begin to feel comfortable with your new view of the world, try a few of these variations.

Get your feet in closer before lifting up. ◇ **Get your hands closer down toward your shoulders before lifting.** ◇ **Once you're up try to walk your hands and feet closer together.** ◇ **Before you begin tie a ribbon around an ankle with a loose, easy knot and try to untie it with your teeth.** ◇

Walk around the room frontwards and backwards (not at the same time!).

PEOPLE WITH BACK PROBLEMS GO TO THE "GUIDE."

As usual be sure that you don't tire yourself too much before you get yourself back down to earth. You don't want to damage your head. Seriously, don't ever do this one around anyone who might think it's funny to tickle you while you're in this position. You obviously could have a terrible accident. One way around it is to have everyone in the room doing it at the same time. Of course they might fall on you. You could lock everybody out! Whatever you do, don't let any animals in the room! A lap in the face at an unexpected moment could finish you.

How about a slightly different approach to this one? See how many times you can push off and lower yourself back to the floor. Push off and then see how many times you can bounce up, relax a little, bounce up, etc. If you're good (this takes more than practice; you have to have the right kind of back) you can take hold of your ankles, from this position, with your hands.

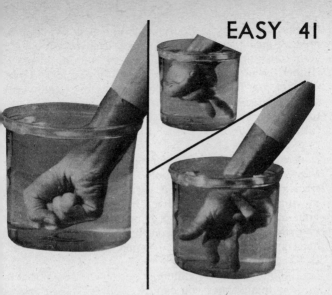

In hot water. ◇ Run a bowl full of water as hot as you can comfortably keep your hand in for a while.

Put your hand in and clench and stretch it a few times to loosen it up. ◇ Now start pulling and folding in one finger at a time, starting with the little finger first, until they are all folded down onto your palm. ◇ Stretch them out as far as you can and then fold them in again, starting with your thumb first this time. ◇ As long as you've got your hand under water, you may as well roll your wrist around first in one direction and then in the other. ◇ Do the same thing with the other hand. ◇ When you take your hands out of the water, dry them briskly and shake and clench them for a while to stir up the circulation even more. ◇ Carry a netsuke, or a small hard rubber ball.

Stiff hands can be miserably uncomfortable. Anything that will stir up your circulation in general will also stir up the circulation in your hands and feet. Walking is great. Jogging, if you can do it, is even better. Shake your hands up overhead. Walking or running in place is fine if you can't get outside (or if they've locked you up after that last bit). Wearing warm gloves and warm socks is an enormous help for people with poor circulation. Don't be so vain that you make yourself uncomfortable or sick. If you have to spend long periods sitting, at least rock!

Poor circulation does not start in your hands and feet; they are attached to your body! People who have poor circulation also quite often get arthritis. Get yourself moving! You're killing yourself by sitting still! Clapping your hands is really quite a good exercise for those of you who are really stiff in your hands. Shake them overhead a little first, though, or it may sting.

Get and keep moving!

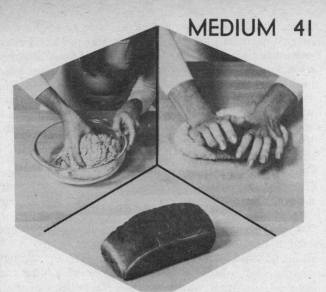

In the dough. ◇ Run water across your wrist until it feels just slightly warm. ◇ Measure out two cups of it into a two-quart bowl. ◇ Add one tablespoon (one package) of baking yeast to the water and stir it a little. ◇ In another bowl add one teaspoon of salt to about three cups of whole-wheat flour and mix it well. ◇ Now start adding the flour mixture to the warm water, until the whole mess leaves the sides of the bowl and forms a sort of soft ball. (Use more flour if you need it.) ◇ Sprinkle a little flour on a board or on the table and turn the ball of dough out onto it. ◇ Sprinkle a little more flour on top of the ball. ◇ Make sure your hands are dry, rub them with a little flour, and knead the ball of dough until it becomes unsticky (about ten minutes). ◇ Turn it often as you knead it and add more flour as necessary to keep it from sticking to the table. ◇ Let it rise until it is double the size it was after kneading and put it in a 325-degree oven for an hour or until it's done. ◇ Turn it out on a rack to cool.

There should always be a large measure of satisfaction in any exercise that is really necessary. What greater sense of accomplishment could there be than not only to make and knead the bread but then to smell it baking?

Don't eat it! Get to be the kind of neighbor everyone wants to have. Give it away! Tomorrow you can make another loaf. And every loaf will help your hands. You'll find after a while that you can turn out a finished (baked, even!) loaf of bread in under an hour. Practice does it—and practice is what you need!

If you're anxious for the bread to bake quickly, make it into very small loaves, or even rolls, and the baking time gets shorter and shorter.

And you get the added benefit of cleaning up the things used, in nice, hot water.

A lot of good bakers use their hands even for the beginning of the bread making, when you're adding the flour to the yeast water. Try it—it's really fun and, again, good for your hands!

Teach all the local kids how to make bread!

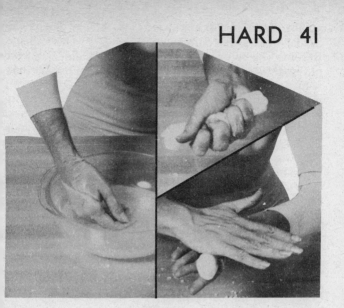

In the waxworks. ◊ First you buy some paraffin. Honest! ◊ Soften it until you can work the whole mess with your fingers. If you get it even softer so that it coats your hands, that's fine.

But it's also very hot. Be careful!

Now you just start working it with your hands —kneading, pulling, rolling, pushing, molding, squeezing, wringing, balling, pounding, anything you can think of. ◊ Use both hands!

Do all this until it becomes too cool to handle at all. But keep it up as long as you can. The harder it gets to handle, the better it's going to be for your hands.

Do you have poor circulation in your hands? Do you have arthritis in your hands and fingers? Do you have stiff joints in your hands? This exercise will not only add heat to relax all the ligaments and muscles and stir up the circulation but will also give you progressively harder work as the paraffin cools.

Become a sculptor, as you improve your hands. It's a lot of fun and you'll be surprised how good you can become with time. If you're going to be doing it every day you may as well enjoy it. If you make something really good, stick it in the refrigerator and keep it . . . and melt down the next batch to use. Make gifts for all your friends, or voodoo dolls of your enemies.

The way to keep hands movable is to keep them moving. The way to stiffen them more is to keep them still. *That is the plain truth!* Handy hints: Knit, sew, write, crochet, type, fiddle . . .

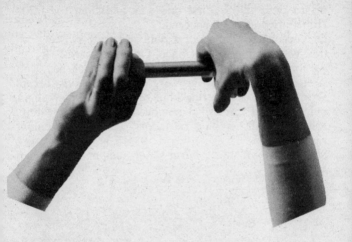

Do this standing, sitting, or lying down. ◊ Take hold of the stiffest doorknob you can find with your right hand.

Turn it as far as you can and back again. ◊ Keeping hold, let your hand tightly slide around as far as possible. ◊ Shift to your left hand, and again turn it as far in one direction as you can and then in the other.

DON'T DO ANYTHING THAT HURTS OR STRAINS!

A lot of people lose strength in their hands without ever realizing what an easy thing it is to get back. You can find different ways of building your strength back up.

A plain table leg works just as well here. Find one that is strong and whose leg you can wrap your hand around. If it's small enough maybe you could take hold of one leg with one hand and another with your other hand. The angle may matter if you're after some specific

327

action, but for the most part, the more different angles you can get it from, the better. Really grab tightly and try to twist it off. First one way and then the other. Hopefully you won't succeed.

Or you can grab hold of a pole and try a twisting motion with both hands at once. Or a chair arm!

As long as you're trying a little harder each day, your strength is going to grow. *Don't hold your breath!* Women used to get this kind of action from wringing out clothes. I can still remember my mother's beautiful arms from all her physical labors. The muscles embarrassed her!

Stiff hands will need warm-water soaking and stretching first.

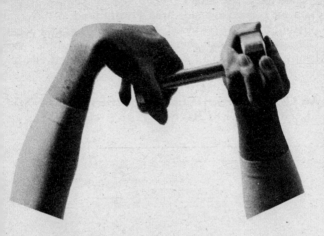

Do this exercise from any position. ◇ Find the
stiffest doorknob you can. ◇ Open the door so
that the edge of it faces you. ◇ Take hold of one
knob with your right hand and the other with your
left.

Using a little pressure, try to turn the knob with
one hand while you resist with the other. ◇ Let
your hands slowly turn, but with some resistance
from each other. ◇ Then reverse the twisting of
the knob. ◇ One hand turns forward while the
other turns back. Then vice versa.

Again, some substitutes for the doorknobs: perhaps an
old towel to twist. It needs to be thick enough to be a
good handful. Some countries still provide a good substitute with their whole long loaves of bread. How about
finding a friend and trying your strength against his?
First his left hand against your right hand and then the
reverse. It's not going to help very much if he's much
stronger than you. Find someone who's pretty evenly

matched against you. If you want to feel really good, find somebody weaker! There are all kinds of things around for you to attack.

You may, if your hands aren't really used to this kind of stuff, break a few blood vessels when you first begin. Don't worry about them; they'll heal. In time your hands will become a lot stronger, blood vessels and all. *Keep at it!*

ARTHRITICS SHOULD DO STRETCHING, NOT CLENCHING, EXERCISES.

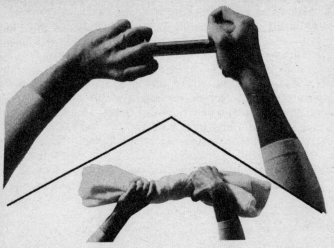

Do this exercise from any position. ◇ Find the stiffest doorknob you can. ◇ Open the door so that the edge of it faces you. ◇ Take hold of one knob with your right hand and take hold of the other knob with your left.

Now really resist hard as you turn your hands as hard as you can against the pressure or resistance of each other. ◇ Reverse the action by turning the other hand forward while the other one goes back.

Put all your strength into it, but don't tear off the door-knobs! Maybe you'd better use a towel! Telephone books, anyone?

Strange things can happen to the hands and feet over very long periods of time. The way the muscles are laid in is pretty much the same for both the hands and the feet. The feet now use their muscles almost entirely to carry and support us properly in standing and moving.

That is a move backwards, in a way, for them. There was a time when they were much more flexible and useful. The hands have gone in the opposite direction. They now no longer (hardly ever) have to support our body weight, and have become much more flexible and sensitive, capable of very refined or intricate movements.

Instead of all four doing the same types of jobs, the hands and the feet now specialize. But there are still people who paint or write with their toes. A friend of mine named Chris once told me that when he was a child and really loving his piano lessons, he was so afraid something might happen to his hands that he tried to learn how to play the piano with his toes also. He probably could do it in a few dozen generations.

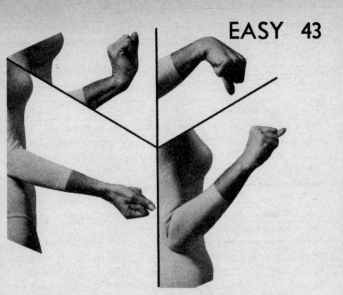

Do this exercise standing or sitting. ◊ Start with your arm hanging loosely at your side.

Twist your fist as far as you can to one side and as far as you can to the other, keeping your elbow at your side.

If you are not used to this much movement in your lower arm you may hear some crunching and cracking. Quit immediately! Then do it for the first few times only under water and only a few times to begin with. Be sure to get your elbow under water also.

Continue to twist your fist from side to side as you bend your elbow and slowly raise your arm until it's against your shoulder. ◊ Twist it also as you lower it to your side again. ◊ Do the same thing with the other arm. ◊ Repeat the movement with your wrist turned back as far as possible, and then with your wrist turned forward as far as possible.

If you feel any pain at all, work up to that point, skip around it, and go on. If you get closer to it every day, it will slowly disappear. You can also try it under very warm water after soaking your arm to the elbow for a while.

There are somewhere around 206 bones in the full-grown human skeleton. Fifty-eight of them are in your two forearms and hands (from the elbow down).

Your eyes and ears and nose let you sense there's an outside world. Your hands allow you to handle it in another way. But your hands and fingers are also very delicate sensing organs. They can tell you the weight, size, shape, texture, temperature, consistency of any object within reaching distance.

When you lose the ability to reach out to test the world, you lose a large part of reality. The more easily you can reach out and handle all things, the more real the world seems; but when reaching and touching become uncomfortable, it is not the world but your discomfort that you are aware of.

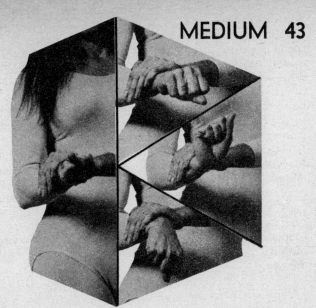

Do this exercise standing or sitting. ◊ Start with one arm hanging loosely by your side. Keep the elbow of the hanging arm at your side throughout the exercise. ◊ Put your other hand on the wrist of the hanging arm. ◊ Make a fist with the hand of your hanging arm. ◊ Press down with the hand that's around your wrist as you raise your other arm.

Twist your fist as far as you can to one side and as far as you can to the other, while you slowly raise that arm (by bending your elbow) to touch your shoulder. ◊ Lower it slowly the same way, twisting your fist from side to side as you apply downward pressure from the other hand. ◊ Do the same thing with the other arm. ◊ Don't forget the variations: wrist turned way back, wrist turned way forward.

DO NOTHING THAT HURTS!

Somehow this seems to me to be an exercise that you should do in your spare time, or when you have to spend time sitting. If you've got good friends who wouldn't misunderstand the motions involved, you could do it while talking. It does cover many different types of movement for the hand and wrist and elbow. Add on to these the pressure from your other arm, and slowly over a period of time you'll find your arms really gaining in strength and flexibility.

Don't exercise only! It would be much better for you, for your arms, for your life in general if you chose things to do that would keep your arms strong and flexible. Brushing your hair is great! Using cast-iron pans is a natural! Braiding hair is a good one. Braiding rugs, knitting, crocheting, needlepoint, shelling peas, preparing green beans, milking cows, catching, carrying, pushing, pulling, throwing, lifting. Keep *in touch* with the world.

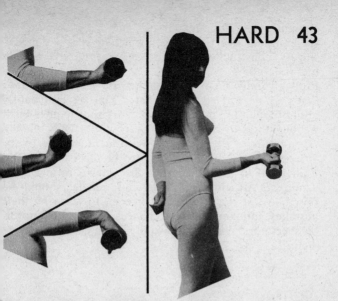

Do this exercise standing or sitting. ◇ Start with one arm hanging loosely by your side. ◇ Put an easy weight to lift in that hand.

Twist your hand with the weight in it as far from side to side as you can. ◇ Now start slowly raising your arm, keeping your elbow at your side, as it bends to lift your twisting hand up to your shoulder. ◇ Lower it again, still twisting. ◇ Do the same thing with the other arm. ◇ Increase the weights as you can or as you want to. ◇ Try it both with your wrist bent back and with your wrist bent forward.

DO THIS ONLY AFTER DOING THE EASIER VERSIONS.

Beautifully muscled arms are a pleasure to look at and to watch at work.
Everyone is attracted by a beautiful body in motion. Isn't it strange that while we are buying more and more

equipment to do our physical labor for us, we are spending our free time gained watching sports, dancers, singers, construction workers, and anyone else we can find in motion?

Probably only men will want to use this exercise, so that's whom I'm addressing here. You see that babies are born with the urge to move. Very shortly after birth we begin saying to them: "Keep still," "Stay there," "Don't run," "Be careful." We train them *not* to try different things! We train them to be *too cautious!* We train them to *be still!* Is this the way to raise an adventurer? All children, male and female, should be raised to test the world they live in, to learn by their mistakes, to take intelligent chances, to live life—not to be spectators! You too! Live life—don't be just an exerciser!

Stand with your back to a very sturdy armchair, wooden if possible. ◊ Put your hands on the arms of the chair.

Bend your knees slightly. ◊ With all your weight on your arms, lower yourself into the chair. ◊ Don't let yourself fall. Practice until you can lower yourself very slowly and evenly.

First time? Please put a pillow on the seat of the chair!

IF YOU HAVE ARTHRITIS, BURSITIS, RHEU-MATISM, OR ANY OTHER KIND OF JOINT PROBLEMS IN YOUR SHOULDERS, ARMS, AND HANDS, CHOOSE GENTLER EXERCISES FROM THE "GUIDE."

If this is the first time you've used this part of your arm in a while, don't worry if you come down with a "plop" the first few tries. That's why I suggested the pillow!

But do keep trying until you can do it slowly and without the emergency drop.

If you think the drop is *too* far, try sitting and with your hands on the chair arms try to raise yourself. Your hands must be no farther forward on the arms of the chair than by the side of your rib cage. If it's *still* too hard, just put your hands on the chair seat behind your bottom, and try to lift yourself up a little. *If that last exercise is just right for you, you're not using your arms nearly enough and need to do this exercise more often.*

This motion gets your shoulders, arms, and hands all at once, but especially the backs of your upper arms.

Do just once or twice the first day or so.

This exercise is probably a ladies' "special." Men, ordinarily, tend to be much stronger through the shoulders than women. But not always!

tand with your back to a very sturdy armchair,
our hands on the arms of the chair, knees slightly
ent.

Vith all your weight on your arms, lower yourself
o the hardest point (you'll feel it in your arms),
nd raise and lower yourself just an inch or two,
ever allowing yourself to touch the seat until your
rms are close to letting go. ◊ Then lower gently.

---

ever just let go—even if you still have the pillow on
he seat.

HOULDER PROBLEMS? LOOK IN THE
GUIDE."

ow that you've come this far, be sure you're using
our legs *only* for balance and not for support. See if
ou're strong enough to raise and lower yourself com-
letely, using just your arms, shoulders, and hands; you

will also feel it, of course, in your upper back an
chest.

Use this exercise and its easier variations only t
strengthen the backs of the upper arms and the variou
other places already mentioned. Don't let yourself fa
into the habit of using this method to get into and ou
of chairs instead of using your thigh muscles. You
arms *should* be able to lift your body, but your legs ce
tainly *must* be kept strong enough to *always* be able t
run you around. Don't weaken them!

Be especially careful if you hear any grating sounds i
your hands, arms, or shoulders. Stop for the day an
wait to see if you develop any aches in the noisy joint
Most often the noise means nothing—but play it saf
If anything *does* ache, soak it in a good hot tub! *Afte*
it recovers, try a gentler exercise.

Stand with your back to a very sturdy armchair, your hands on the arms of the chair, knees slightly bent, with all your weight on your arms.

Lower yourself slowly onto the chair. ◇ Rise slowly to support yourself on your straightened arms —knees still bent. ◇ Lower and raise yourself as slowly and steadily as possible as many times as possible. ◇ Only a few the first time, please! ◇ Too easy? Raise your legs straight out in front as you raise and lower yourself!

EASIER VERSIONS FIRST!

Here again, of course, you're exercising the hands and shoulders, and using the shoulders, you're automatically getting your upper back and chest muscles.
Now add to that—if you can (I can't!)—the horizontally raised legs, and you're working your abdominals and your thighs at the same time as all the other muscles!

I know a seventy-one-year-old man who can do this! Condition matters—not age!

Although men tend to be stronger than women through the shoulders, a female acrobat or mountain climber is going to be more capable of doing this exercise than a male in poor condition.

Try not to be too cautious with children. Weakness is almost always much more dangerous than a few small accidents. We all learn by making mistakes. We should learn to try a different way, not to quit trying! Let them climb!

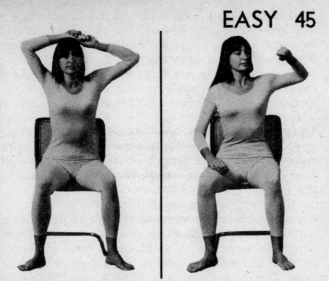

Do this exercise sitting in a chair.

This is a very easy version for you if you have real problems getting your arms up overhead.

Clasp your hands in your lap.

Bring both hands up to the top of your head. ◇ **Bring one arm back down to your lap.** ◇ **With the other arm still bent, let it down very slowly, giving it little bounces back about every quarter inch down that you come, until it is down at your side.** ◇ **Repeat the whole exercise, but this time use the other arm.**

If you lose your balance easily, try doing this one sitting far forward in a chair, legs planted far apart. When you feel you can, someday, try bouncing the arm back up again. Hurt? Use your other arm to help support you past any uncomfortable spots. Be very gentle. If you are very stiff it will take time.

345

It's horrible to feel helpless! Don't just sit there if you can do anything at all to help yourself. Even a rocking chair and knitting is a great deal better than nothing! Your joints are rusting away!

If you haven't done anything for a long time why not try just lifting your arms up a little way today? Tomorrow you can lift them a little higher. Or try this:

Clasp your hands in your lap, lift them up a little way, and pull your right arm way around with your left arm to the left. ◊ Then change and pull your left arm way around with your right arm to the right.

As you get stronger you will be able to raise them higher and higher. Don't let one day go by without moving in some way! Your shoulder joints are meant to have an enormous amount of freedom to move in many directions. If you have allowed your body to get so stiff that it can no longer move in the world, you now must live only inside your body! Unless you are willing to fight for your freedom!! Start using your body in any way you can think of! Wash windows, scrub floors, clean the walls, do the dishes—any experience is beautiful compared to no experience!

**Stand with your feet placed well apart for balance.
◊ Clasp your hands together in front of you.**

**Lift your arms up so that they are overhead with
the elbows straight. ◊ Lower one arm. ◊ With
the arm that is overhead, start making little
bounces back, back, back, and then lower it down
to your side little by little, making sure to bounce
it constantly. ◊ If you can, raise it up the same
way. ◊ Then do the other arm.**

If you hit a painful spot, work up to it, move beyond it,
and start working again just the other side of the painful area. In time you will probably find that it will disappear. Be patient and don't force anything.

**THIS EXERCISE CAN REALLY HURT BAD
NECKS. TAKE IT VERY EASY, AND IF YOU
HAVE ANY DOUBTS AT ALL ASK YOUR DOC-
TOR.**

The upper end of your arm bone, where it becomes a part of the shoulder joint, is shaped like a ball. Cartilage covers this ball where it fits into the socket. Cartilage is one kind of connecting tissue . . . the most elastic kind. On this bone it is a little thicker in the center than at the outside edges, making it a little rounder. The socket it fits into also is lined with cartilage, but here it is a little thinner in the center of the socket and a little thicker at the outside edges, making it a little deeper. Pushing, pulling, and twisting take a very complicated shoulder joint. Though difficult to explain, if you use it—move, stretch, reach, and twist— there is no better, nor more appreciative, servant than your own body. It becomes more and more alive, healthier, and more beautiful with every new job you give it to do . . . if it is fed well at the same time!

Condition your arms, hands, shoulders, neck, and hair all at the same time: Brush your hair (women *and* men) a hundred strokes every night. Staying in shape can save you thousands of dollars.

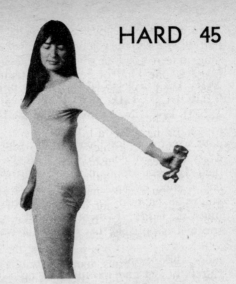

Stand with your feet planted well apart for balance.

Don't use weights when you try this exercise for the first time.

Have your arms hanging at your sides.

Swing your right arm up overhead and back as far as possible. ◇ **Do not bend your elbow! Do not put too much strain on the joint!** ◇ **Swing your arm back down in an even swing to your side again.** ◇ **Now swing it back up again, but just a little farther out to the side, and then back down to your side.** ◇ **Swing it up again, still a little more out to the side, and back down.** ◇ **Keep it up until you have completed the semicircle, from up overhead to down by your side.** ◇ **Do the same thing with the other arm.**

If nothing hurts *then* you can try the same exercise with *very* light weights! Keep them light for this exercise and don't get too rambunctious! You have nothing to lose but your shoulder!

DON'T DO THIS EXERCISE AT ALL UNTIL YOU HAVE WORKED YOUR WAY AT LEAST THROUGH THE MEDIUM VERSION. START WITH THE LIGHTEST OF WEIGHTS.

This exercise is for those of you who are working for every last bit of flexibility you can get from your shoulders. Baseball, football, javelin throwing, shot-putting, any number of sports will use your arm this way. If you're in shape for them when you begin the season, so much the better. If you are doing it as conditioning for a sport, it is possible that you might want to put a little

more work into it.

Carefully and under control, swing a little more freely. If you are really being *very* careful, try adding just a little more weight every day, for a while. This is not a competitive sport! You are only working against yourself! Take your time. You can get almost anywhere you want to with patience and time.

Keep away from open and closed doors while practicing this one. It would be murder for someone to run into!

Don't do exercises for extreme flexibility without also doing some to strengthen the *muscles* in this area also. Otherwise you are *not in good shape!* Strengthen *and* stretch!

NEVER THROW YOUR ARM IN AN UNCON-TROLLED MANNER. ESPECIALLY NOT WITH A WEIGHT IN YOUR HAND! NOT ONLY YOUR SHOULDER BUT ALSO YOUR ELBOW IS AT STAKE.

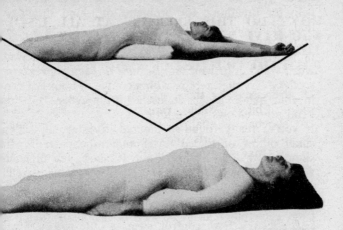

Lie on your back, with a pillow low down under the shoulders.

Breathe in and relax as you bring your arms up overhead to touch the floor behind your head. ◇ Try to keep your elbows straight! ◇ Breathe out with a "kh" sound and push down hard with your abdominal muscles as you bring your arms, head, and shoulders up from the floor and your arms over and down to your sides. ◇ Elbows straight again!

Raise the foot of the bed as the exercise gets easier for you to do.

ARE YOUR SHOULDERS TIGHT? LOOK IN THE "GUIDE."

As you bring your arms up overhead to touch the floor, you are stretching all the tissue that connects your ribs to your spine in back and to your breast bone—the

351

bone right in the middle of your chest in front. This
makes your rib cage more flexible and lifts it up—a big
help for breathing, for problems of round shoulders
and for abdominal problems—all from one simple exercise! And it helps straighten the hump some of us acquire from letting our head and shoulders drop forward
when walking or working. *Be sure to keep your elbows
straight!* Try the exercise with a couple of books or cans
in your hands. Makes it just a little tougher. But now
bend your elbows just a little.

If you're really round-shouldered, try sleeping with a
small pillow or folded towel under the part of your
shoulders that tends to stick out. It takes a few nights to
get used to, but then it won't bother you. It will stretch
you out.

Move rhythmically! Stretch legs and arms hard away
from each other as your arms come up overhead! It
feels great!

Lie on your back across a bed. ◊ **Your head, neck, and shoulders should be hanging over the edge, arms back overhead touching the floor.**

Stretch hard! ◊ **Breathe out with a "kh" sound and push down hard with your abdominal muscles as you bring your arms, head, and shoulders up from the floor and your arms over to your sides.**

Watch it! *Don't fall off on your head!*

DO THE EASIER VERSION FIRST!

The farther over the edge of the bed you let your head and shoulders hang, the harder this exercise will be! Coming up with your head and shoulders and swinging back over the edge of the bed to touch your hands to the floor will be more difficult—*and do you more good,* unless you've got a slippery spread, or are *too far* over the edge! *Please be careful!* If the regular way is a little too tough for you, just wiggle yourself farther up onto the bed. The *less* you have hanging over the *easier* it will be!

This weird position can be a real help for pregnant women! When the baby starts kicking you in the lungs, there's only one thing you can do—*move out of the way!* Or if you feel you'd just like to take a really full breath again, this is the way!

And for double chins! Don't trust me—put your hands around the front of your neck as you come up. *Feel that?*

Be sure to breathe out as you come up and in as you go back down! Slowly and rhythmically! As you breathe out—bear down hard!

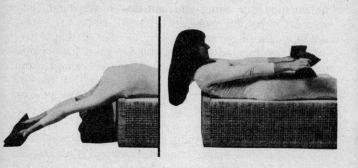

Lie on your back across a bed. ◇ Hold a two-pound can in each hand. ◇ Your head, neck, and shoulders should be hanging back over the edge, hands lying on the bed at your side.

Breathe in as you bring your arms up overhead and way down to the floor behind your head. ◇ Stretch as far back as possible. ◇ Breathe out with a "kh" sound and push down hard with your abdominal muscles at the same time as you raise your head, neck, and shoulders up level with the bed or a little higher and bring your arms up, over, and to your sides on the bed again. ◇ Increase the weights slowly.

Be sure when you're using something for a weight that you can get a firm grip on it. Remember, if you have adjustable weights, to check to see that they're tight each time you use them.

NOT FOR YOU IF YOU HAVE A HERNIA!

Take slippery spreads off the bed before attempting this one. Don't get too far over the edge to begin with. If you feel at all like you're in a dangerous position, work your way back up onto the bed a little farther. With the weights in your hands, if you slipped, you could give yourself some real problems!

When you've been working long enough so that a two-pound can feels too light, you will probably have a time trying to find a heavier weight that you can get your hand around well enough to hold it safely. But be sure that you do! Sometimes you can buy adjustable weights, second hand.

If the method of breathing suggested in this exercise is too much for you to do at the same time as you're using the weights, if it makes your head ache, if it makes you dizzy, or if it makes your pulse speed up much, shift back to breathing with your mouth open. *Don't hold your breath at all!* If any of these things do happen, it's best to get your blood pressure checked. If your blood pressure is okay, slow down in the amount of weight you're trying to lift.

In any case the weights should always be completely under your control. If they are too heavy for you to lower to the floor behind your head, slowly and steadily, they are too heavy for you to use!

Your purpose here is to stretch and compress the walls of the chest, and to stretch and develop the abdominals. You do not need a terribly heavy weight to accomplish this. Start with small weights and don't work up too far. Maybe fifteen pounds at the most for women, twenty-five at the most for men, unless it's for some special purpose, such as trapeze work or mountain climbing.

Guard your shoulder joint well! Start slowly, work your way up in pounds of weight slowly, and don't try to do too much in one day! You can do almost anything you choose if you'll just be cautious.

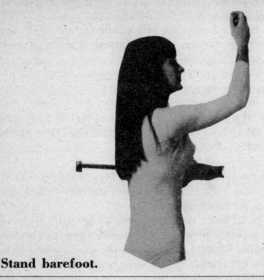

Stand barefoot.

Put twelve papers, each one marked with a number from one to twelve, in a circle around you on the floor, like a clock—with twelve o'clock straight ahead and six o'clock behind you. You can make the circle as large or as small as you want, according to the space you have.

Place your legs a little apart for balance and have your arms hanging freely at your sides. ◊ If you're in very bad shape, hang on to something like the side of a sink with your left arm while working with your right.

Swing your right arm once very loosely and gently across in front of you and up a little directly toward nine o'clock, and let it swing naturally back. If your elbow bends a little on this easiest version, don't worry. ◊ Swing once toward nine, then to ten and so on all the way around to eight (behind you). ◊ Then swing your left arm toward three and continue swinging slowly and gently toward each number until you've swung all the way around in back toward four.

If you feel little or no discomfort, after the first day, slowly increase the number of times that you swing toward each number. Take it easy, and stop if you get tired. Breathe normally.

IF YOU HAVE A SHOULDER PROBLEM, BE SURE TO ASK YOUR DOCTOR'S PERMISSION BEFORE BEGINNING.

Everyone needs to begin with this easy version; even if you think you're in good condition you may find it will bother you in some ways.

If at any point your shoulder hurts while you are doing it—stop! Swing only to those points you can reach without pain. When you come to the point where you know from experience that it will begin to hurt—stop! Move around that point and continue. Keep this up every day, moving closer little by little to the uncomfortable point until finally, one day, according to your condition, you'll ease right through it with hardly any discomfort at all. Take your time. Don't push it. *But do keep your shoulder moving! Don't miss a day! Be patient and consistent!*

When you are able to move through the position that was painful be sure you continue to handle this movement gently and carefully for a while. You can ruin the whole step forward by getting too enthusiastic and doing *too much!* The most important thing you can do for a stiff or frozen shoulder is to get it moving again. Start as slowly as you want to—*but start!*

Stand barefoot.

Put twelve papers, each one marked with a number
from one to twelve, in a circle around you on the floor,
like a clock—with twelve o'clock straight ahead and six
o'clock behind you. Make the circle any size, or imagine
it.

**Place your legs a little apart for balance, arms
hanging freely by your sides.**

**Now make believe the clock is up overhead and
swing your right arm way up high directly toward
nine o'clock and let it swing naturally back. Try to
keep your elbow as straight as possible, but not
stiff. ◇ Swing high up toward each number, all
the way around to eight (behind you), and then
swing your left arm high up directly toward three
and all the way around to four (behind you).**

If your shoulders feel fine the next day, try swinging up
twice toward each number or try doing it a little more

enthusiastically. If anything ever hurts, stop immediately, and swing much more gently for a while.

YOU SHOULD BE COMPLETELY FREE OF PAIN IN YOUR SHOULDER JOINT BEFORE YOU BEGIN THIS VERSION.

Your upper arm bone has a knob on the end that fits into a hollowed-out section on the outside edge of your "wing" bone. If you put one fist into your other hand and curl that hand around it, you have a vague idea how it's set up. The curled hand would be the shoulder socket and the fist would be the ball on the end of your arm bone (or humerus).

The scapula, or "wing," helps enormously to give freedom of movement to the shoulder by turning and twisting in order to put the socket that is on its edge in the best position possible for the job it has to do. Feel the "wing" as you move your arm. To cap it all off, there are muscles coming off in all directions from the shoulder joint to give it the strength and flexibility needed. You are walking around in nothing less than a work of art! Take good care of it!

Stand barefoot.

Put twelve papers, each one marked with a number from one to twelve, in a circle around you on the floor, like a clock—with twelve o'clock straight in front of you and six o'clock directly behind. Once you've got the idea you really don't have to put the papers there every day. Just imagine it. But imagine it up overhead.

Place your feet apart for balance, and have your arms hanging freely but with small weights of equal size in each hand.

Swing your right arm way up high and directly toward nine o'clock and let it swing naturally back. Try to keep your elbow as straight as possible, but not stiff! ◇ Swing high up toward each number all the way around to eight (behind you) and then swing your left arm high up directly toward three and all the way around to four (behind you).

Don't go into this one too enthusiastically. Go easy on your joints. Just a little more swing each day, a little more weight in each hand each day.

DO THIS ONLY AFTER THE EASIER VERSIONS HAVE BECOME EASY.

The shoulder socket is capable of being pulled apart from one to two inches. All sorts of elastic tissue make this safely possible in a healthy shoulder. Good flexibility is not something you should expect of your shoulder joint if you have not been doing the right kind of steady physical activity. Baseball, football, and lacrosse players should have no difficulty at all with this exercise *if* they have been practicing.

If you need conditioning for your shoulder you certainly will need it for your elbow also. Check the "guide." The use of weights with this exercise immediately puts an added strain on your elbow, especially since you are using a swinging motion. Take it easy! *Be sure that you start with a very light weight and work your way up very slowly over a long period of time.*

Be sure that you have a firm grip on the weights, and that no one is standing close by. You should also stay away from doorways, in case someone decides to come in suddenly.

Last but not least, keep the weights away from places where young children might happen on them. They can do terrible damage when dropped on toes. Best yet, use bean bags in various weights. They're much safer!

If your shoulder aches after this one, try soaking in a hot tub, shoulders under the water, of course.

Sit down.

Roll one of your shoulders around in a small and gentle circle. ◇ **First forward and then back.** ◇ **Do the other shoulder.** ◇ **Only once in either direction the first day.**

GO GENTLY WITH INJURED SHOULDERS! ASK YOUR DOCTOR.

Try this exercise for stiff shoulders, or a stiff neck, either from working, tenseness, or extreme cold, to ease up the shoulders and neck you have not been using, or have not been using properly. Try it with your eyes closed. This is one of those special "goodies." Feel good?

If you happen to be one of those people who hunch their shoulders up when they get nervous, try practicing this several times a day. Or if you have to spend much time peering at a typewriter or papers on a desk in front of you, you'll find this a great relief. This is a good beginning exercise for people who are recovering from bursitis. It is also great for arthritics—not too tough.

If you have been having a lot of pain from shoulder-joint problems, try soaking in a hot tub for a while before trying the shoulder movement. Even more helpful would be doing it while the shoulder is still in the hot water. Try to have that shoulder completely free to move, but still immersed. That in itself is a pretty good trick!

Sit on the floor.

Roll both your shoulders at once around in the biggest circle you can. ◊ **Now roll them back in the other direction.** ◊ **Try rolling them faster.** ◊ **Try rolling one up as the other goes down.**

CAUTION: IF YOU HAVE ARTHRITIS, BURSITIS, OR WHIPLASH, SPEAK TO YOUR DOCTOR BEFORE TRYING THIS!

If you have had bursitis, stay with the easy version of this exercise for a good long while before coming to this —especially if you have any lingering discomfort.
Just in case you didn't know, "itis" means inflammation. "Arthr-" means joint. "Bursa-" means purse (it's a purse of fluid meant to protect your softer tissues from having to ride constantly across a bare bone). To irritate the inflammation further by exercising immediately after an injury is certainly not going to stop your discomfort. On the other hand, you don't want to be

permanently at rest! The answer is to rest the affected area for a while, days or weeks according to what your doctor says, and then slowly (preferably under water) get it moving again. Whatever you do, don't give the part that hurts a long enough rest so that it begins to deposit calcium.

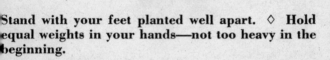

Stand with your feet planted well apart. ◊ **Hold equal weights in your hands—not too heavy in the beginning.**

Roll your shoulders around in a big circle, first in one direction, then in the other. ◊ **Increase the weights as you can, day by day.**

IT'S IMPORTANT THAT YOU DO THE EASIER VERSIONS FIRST!

Everyone has at least seen pictures of the shoulder yokes that are used to carry a heavy load. Our shoulders are set up in very much the same way, but with the yoke on backwards. This arrangement allows you to carry evenly balanced and heavy loads without putting a great strain on the rib cage.

Take a weight (not too large) in each hand. Put one down and watch what happens to your shoulder. Pick it up again, and, standing with your feet planted well, start rolling your shoulders around in a circle. Then roll

them around in the opposite direction. As you ge
stronger use heavier and heavier weights.

You'll find that as the weights get heavier it is easier t
carry them in close with your arms bent. Weights to
heavy or too bulky for your arms will feel quite com
fortable when lifted up onto your shoulders. But fo
this exercise, letting the weights hang is exactly right
You are *trying* to increase the work load to strengthe
your shoulders in just this area, in just this way.

Stand barefoot. ◊ **Hold a doubled-up pillow between your lower arm and your chest.**

Press the pillow in gently and firmly until your arm is pulled close to your chest. If it's painful, do it even more gently. ◊ **Try it at a little higher angle or at a little lower angle.** ◊ **Try it first with your fist turned up and then with your fist turned under.** ◊ **When you can do it easily, breathe out with a "kh" sound and bear down hard as you pull the pillow in.** ◊ **Breathe in as you relax.**

One of the muscles most neglected by people who are trying to strengthen and develop themselves is the "sub-scapularis," which means the muscle under the wing bone (scapula). It is attached quite broadly across the underside of the wing bone and then comes up and around to attach to the front of the shoulder joint, to the small bony projection of the arm bone and to the wrappings of the shoulder joint itself.

This muscle is quite often injured at the point where it

is attached in front. A strong pull back for a throw of any sort or any movement that pulls the shoulder back violently can tear it slightly loose from its moorings. It should be *gently* stretched out (look in the "guide") in training for any sport that requires this move, and it should also be strengthened.

This is a series of exercises that will develop and strengthen it. If you have injured it, heat, massage, and a gentle beginning of exercise under water will do a lot of good. Don't try to improve too fast if you *have* injured it. This will only serve to tear the muscle more or to give you a chronically painful condition. If this muscle is injured, be sure to do stretching exercises also! Gently!

Sit on the floor. ◊ Your knees bent and your feet on the floor. ◊ Your feet should be out a little way, your arms around your knees.

Start pulling with your arms while at the same time you resist with your legs. ◊ Pull as hard as you can and slowly allow your legs to be pulled in close. ◊ Breathe out with a "kh" sound and bear down hard with your belly muscles as you pull in on your knees, and you'll find you can also be doing some very good abdominal work! ◊ Breathe in as you let your knees slide out to begin again.

This is a very good exercise!

NO HERNIAS!

This begins to feel like work. As you first begin, be sure to test to see that your muscle is not in too weak a condition to take the pulling you're going to give it. Develop the pull *gradually!* You can end up *putting* a terrific amount into this one. Try it with your wrists turned up first, then with your wrists turned out, then with them turned down. It may end up being harder for you than the so-called harder variation! If it is, stick with this one. Don't ever let it slip from being a regular exercise if you're involved *in any throwing or slamming motions!*

Be sure to look up and use the exercises that will keep the shoulder joint flexible also. If the body has good flexibility, it is less likely to get stretched far enough to hurt it.

If you have a chronic painful condition involving this muscle, work with the easier versions until you are completely free of pain; then go on to these. Chronic conditions of the muscles and joints can be overcome quite often with time and patience. *Quite often!* Be patient. No violence. If it hurts—stop!

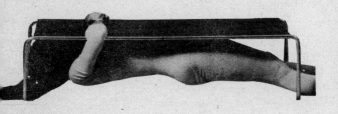

Lie down on your back underneath a strong bench or coffee table. ◊ **Wrap your arms up around it.** ◊ **Keep your body in a straight line from your head to your heels.**

Pull your shoulders and chest up to the table and lower yourself slowly.

TEST IT FIRST! DON'T DO IT IF IT HURTS, OR IF YOUR ARMS ARE WEAK.

This may not be as hard for you as the last exercise. Try them both out to see which one is going to do the most for you.

It is quite true that the circulation and healing of an injured part are increased if that part is kept active. Keeping it too strongly active may just serve to injure it more! *Don't do anything with an injured shoulder that makes it painful without your doctor having advised it!* Do anything else with it that you can, always taking care not to bring it to the point of pain. Discomfort is okay, pain is not!

This exercise is a good one for getting this muscle (the subscapularis) into good muscular condition. Choose one to stretch it out as far as possible also. Never go after only stretching or only developing it! *Always use stretching and strengthening of this muscle in the same conditioning program.* Exercises like this, in which everything is pretty much under control, are great preparation for any activity that uses the shoulders violently.

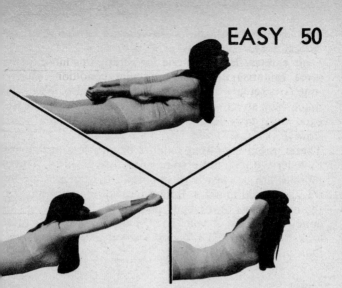

Lie on your belly on a reasonably flat surface, preferably the floor.

A soft bed will not do!

Put your hands behind your back and clasp them.

Lift up your head and shoulders as far as possible. ◇ Hold as long as possible. ◇ Or lift up and down as long as possible. ◇ Then (do only when the first is easy), put your hands behind your head and repeat the motions. ◇ Finally (do only when the others are easy), put your arms out in front of you and repeat the motions.

THIS EXERCISE SHOULD NOT BE DONE BY ANYONE WHO HAS ANY TYPE OF LOW BACK PAIN!

This is an excellent exercise for anyone trying to strengthen back muscles that are *only weak*. No back-injury patients allowed!

Start slowly! In time you can have your back as strong as you could possibly want it. A stiff back is very uncomfortable. If you do too much, and make it ache, don't get excited. Get into a warm tub and soak as much of the ache out as you can. Next time don't do so much! Since you never feel much when you're doing an exercise, it is really easy to do too much. *Don't.* Start slowly!

There are an enormous number of muscle attachments that serve to pull the spine into this position. These muscles are not nearly as important to your posture as the abdominal muscles. But all muscles are important to the movements of the body and should be kept in good condition. Look at *your* back. Do you like the way it looks? Most people's backs are very neglected—*and look it.*

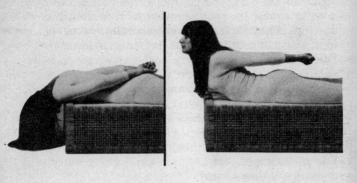

Lie on your belly on your bed. ◇ Your head and shoulders should be just over the edge. ◇ Put your hands behind your back and clasp them.

Lift up your head and shoulders as far as possible. ◇ Hold them up as long as possible. ◇ Or lift up and down as often as possible. ◇ Then (do after the first becomes easy), clasp your hands behind your head and repeat the motions. ◇ Finally (do only after the other two have become easy), put your arms out in front of you and repeat the motions.

NOT FOR BAD BACKS! ONLY BAD-LOOKING BACKS!

You can see that this is just a slight variation on the easier version, making it just a step harder, making your back a little stronger, and a little better to look at. The reason for changing the position of the arms is to put the work on slightly different parts of the back by changing where the weight of the arms is. The farther out the arms go in front, the lower down in the back you get most of the work. The farther *back* they go the higher in the back you get the work. That allows you, now, to choose the spot you want most to strengthen or develop. The whole back is important. Some places look worse than others. Some feel worse than others.

Do you want an easier way out? Follow the kids' example. Lie on the floor on your belly to read, watch television, and make telephone calls. Always make use, bodily, of time that is usually wasted. *Changed habits alone can make you a beautiful body*. How about doing a separate exercise near the telephone, the television, by the sink, in the kitchen, in the bathroom, by the side of your bed, etc.? Wow! Any waking time spent unmoving is time wasted.

Lie on your belly on your bed, with your head and shoulders and as much of your chest and waist as you can get over the edge and still manage to lift your upper body up from the floor. ◇ Put your hands behind you and clasp them.

Lift up your upper body as far as possible. ◇ Hold it up as long as possible. ◇ Lift up and down as often as possible. ◇ Then (do after the first becomes easy), clasp your hands behind your head and repeat the motions. ◇ Finally (do only after the other two have become easy), put your arms out in front of you and repeat the motions.

ONLY FOR BACKS ALREADY IN REASONABLE CONDITION!

The exercises in this series are great for divers, pole vaulters, and anyone who has something to lift, from babies to anything else you can think of, no matter how heavy, no matter how light.

379

Here's a good hint for you: *Never lift anything until you have tested its weight first, and until you have tested to see how it's going to sag or shift as you lift it.* To make these exercises a little or a lot harder, start adding light weights to your hands as soon as the basic ones become easy. *Build up slowly* as always. *Move slowly the first time you use an increased weight. Test it out! It's a lot easier to prevent problems than to recover from them.* If you want to take chances, go out for competitive sports.

If you do get a spasm from going into one of these exercises too quickly, roll over immediately and curl up into a ball. Rock back and forth on your back for a while and try to undo it. Try a hot bath later. Haste makes a doubled-over back.

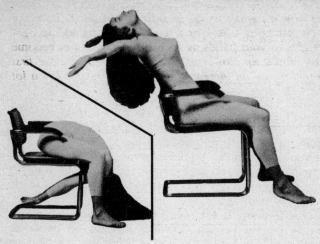

This exercise is to be done sitting.

Choose an armchair whose back ends just under your shoulder blades.

Sit a little forward in the chair, knees far apart for balance, feet well planted on the floor.

Lift your arms up overhead and lean back as far as possible over the back of the chair.

The chair will support you—let your head drop back.

Now lean over forward and to the floor to bring your arms far under the chair—head relaxed! ◊ Try to stretch as much as you can coming up and going over the back of the chair again. ◊ When you have the movement right and feel secure (it doesn't need to be today or even next week), try this variation: As you come up, breathe in. ◊ As you go over, breathe out with a "kh" sound and tighten your belly muscles!

DO YOU HAVE NECK OR SHOULDER PROBLEMS? DON'T DO IT! IF YOU GET DIZZY AT ALL WHEN BENDING FORWARD, DON'T DO IT!

This is a marvelous exercise for those of you who have not bent in the middle for a long time, and for those of you with breathing problems. And it's a good abdominal exercise! And it's a good upper back stretch for those of you with rounded shoulders.

If you're a beginner, go over forward very slowly to test whether your back feels happy with it, and whether you're going to get dizzy. If everything seems to be okay you're all set.

If you're doing it for round shoulders, you can add a pillow behind your back which reaches up to below your shoulder blades. If you're using the exercise for breathing problems, try putting a pillow close in against your lower abdomen and your thighs. Make sure you can come all the way over it. If it's too large, you could try a folded towel. This is a good stretch! Feels marvelous! For breathing problems or just to develop the belly muscles, really tighten your belly hard as you exhale and go over between your legs. Everybody likes this one!

DIZZY? QUIT!

Stand with your feet well apart for balance.

If your balance is bad, don't do this exercise!

Lift your arms way up and back overhead, leaning back as far as possible. ◇ Put your head way back. ◇ Then sweep forward and down between your legs as far as possible and swing right back up in order to stretch back again. ◇ Keep the motion up in a smooth flow. ◇ As you come up breathe in deeply. ◇ As you go over breathe out with a "kh" sound and tighten your belly muscles.

IF YOUR BACK IS BAD, DON'T DO THIS EXERCISE!

Once you have done this exercise for a while and begin to get the swing of it, just relax and enjoy it. It really makes you feel alive! It's one of my favorites. *Be sure not to prevent yourself from leaning far back as you swing up.* And let your head swing under with your body as you go over. *Don't try to look up as you go down!* Try to feel everything that's going on in your body. This exercise always makes me feel as though it's spring! It's funny how movement can change your mood. All up and out movements tend to make·you feel the way they look. You really can condition yourself to feel better with good moves. When you feel bad you naturally tend to curl in on yourself. And when you feel good, you stretch up and out and move in smoother and more satisfying ways. If you're ever feeling downright rotten, try this exercise and see how strange it feels. Weird? Just plain old walking becomes a different thing when you feel good. Notice next time. Is your balance good? Try it with your eyes closed. Feels great!

NOT FOR BAD BACKS.

Stand. ◊ **Have your legs far apart for balance.**

Crouch to put your arms between or at the outside of your legs. ◊ Leap high into the air, stretching your arms far back as your back arches. ◊ Come down on your feet and then quickly crouch down to put your arms between your legs again. It takes a while to work smoothly from the air to the crouch but it feels so beautiful it's worth it. ◊ Again, try to inhale on the way up and exhale on the way down.

ONLY FOR YOU IF YOU'RE IN GOOD SHAPE!

This is the "pure joy" exercise! If you can do this one without smiling or laughing I'll be very much surprised. It does that to you. If you're ever nervous about facing a new situation, try doing a few of these before leaving the house, and then carry the memory and the feeling with you. Nothing can get you down when you're really up!

Do you know that you condition people by the way you look? Lift up your chin, straighten up your back, walk with a spring in your step, no matter how you started out feeling. You'll not only look better, if you look in a mirror, you'll feel better too! So will everyone who looks at you! Lift up! Smile! Make the world feel better. Don't stay inside after doing this exercise. You owe yourself to the world!

Let out a whoop as you leap up. Feels even better!

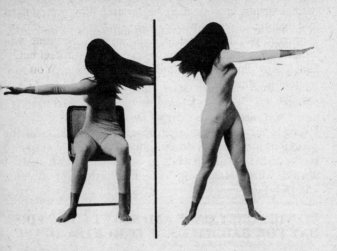

Make sure to move all furniture and friends from your general vicinity first. You can start in a chair if your balance is very bad. If you do start in a chair, put your knees and your feet far apart for balance. A stool or an ottoman would really be better than a chair. Then you wouldn't run into the back as you swing around.

Just hold your arms out loosely at your sides and swing them from side to side. ◊ **Twist your upper body as you swing your arms.** ◊ **If you're going to do it from a standing position, put your feet apart for better balance.** ◊ **Do it the first time slowly to check out your balance. Now you're all ready to go.** ◊ **Just swing easily from side to side.** ◊ **Let your whole upper body and your head swing with it.**

BAD BACKS—TEST IT FIRST!

For trimming and making your waistline flexible, this is a good beginning. Very few people really keep their bodies as flexible as they should be and could be. Your waistline can be as small and as tight as it was when you were in your best condition. If you never were in your best condition, it makes no difference. *You can be in it now!* Honestly. If you're willing to work, no matter what your age or condition (unless of course the exercises cause you pain), *you can get yourself into top condition! But you must start slowly! You must be consistent! And you must choose the right exercises!* It's never too late—or too early! *Do it now!*

Exercise serves a double purpose. It always inspires the people around you to do the same. Wouldn't you like to see your family and friends in better shape? (It doesn't *always* work. Have you seen my husband?) Breathe naturally!

DO THIS ONLY ONCE AND SLOWLY THE FIRST DAY FOR BAD BACKS. IF IT HURTS—QUIT!

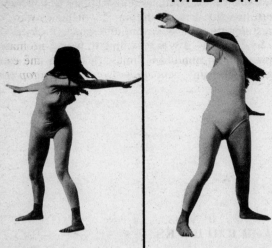

tand barefoot. ◊ Place your feet apart for bal-
nce. ◊ Arch your back and lean a little forward,
rms out to the sides.

wing your arms from side to side as far as pos-
ible. ◊ Keep your head up. ◊ Try it also lean-
ng back, knees bent a little. ◊ Swing side to side.
◊ Let your head follow your arms. ◊ Slowly at
rst! Test it!

'OU WITH THE BAD BACK—DON'T EVEN TRY 'HIS!

'o build flexibility and strength at the same time, you
nly need to bend a little. Leaning forward will build up
he muscles of your back and side-back as you swing
rom side to side. Leaning backward will build up the
nuscles of your front and side abdominals or all around
he front of your waistline. If it bothers your back *at all,*
hoose some other exercise. The easy version, standing,
nay be what you need. My mother used to say, "If

you're capable of bending, you're not likely to break."
I don't think she was talking about bodies, but I like it.
Be careful to move the furniture; it's better to look for
trouble before you (literally) run into it. If you really
swing freely, you can hurt yourself by banging into
something. That's the voice of experience speaking. All
these swinging exercises feel terrific. *Just a few the first
day!*

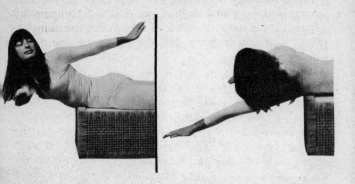

Lie on your bed with your upper body over the edge. ◊ **Face up first.** ◊ **Be as far over as you can be and still hold yourself out straight.**

Swing your arms from side to side.

Gently at first; don't break your fingers!

Then turn over and again get as far over the edge of the bed as you can and still keep your body out straight while you swing your arms from side to side.

If you put your legs far apart, you can keep your balance better. If your bed is too close to the floor, bend your elbows. You can swing further around that way. Try to swing the whole upper part of your body. (Hard!) Follow your arms with your head. Do more with whichever part (front or back) is weakest. See how many times you can do it.

TOO HARD FOR BAD BACKS!

Now you're working against gravity. Pretty rugged when you first start. Don't worry; just move back a little farther on the bed until you get a little stronger. Move out little by little. Your feet are going to keep threatening to leave the bed and dump you (bodily) on the floor.

If you just can't make it with this exercise it's probably because either your back or your abdominal muscles (or both) are simply not strong enough. So do some more back and abdominal exercises until you *can* do this motion. There are lots of other, and easier, exercises to get them into better condition. It's not going to do you any good if you're draped over the edge of the bed like a wet rag. You have to be able to hold your upper body out straight. Besides, if your head is on the floor you can't swing your arms.

If you fall off the bed, remember, I warned you. How about putting a rug at the end of the bed?

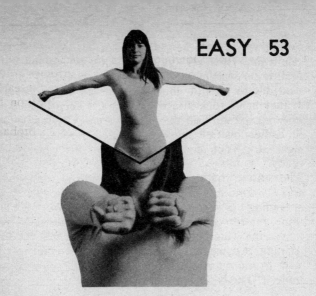

Stand with your feet apart for balance.

You can do this exercise sitting if you want.

Hold your arms out straight ahead at shoulder level. ◊ **Have your fists touching.**

Turn your fists in so that your thumbs are far down and then turn them out, so that the inside of your fist is way up. ◊ **Keep twisting them in and out and, still at shoulder level, move your arms at the same time slowly out to your sides and as far around behind you as you can.** ◊ **Bring them, always twisting, back around to the front.**

SHOULDER-JOINT PROBLEMS? CHOOSE SOMETHING EASIER.

If you tend to have trouble with your shoulder joints, don't start with this exercise. There are easier beginnings for extremely bad shoulder joints that will be

393

gentler for you. If your shoulders are only weak, this one is fine. However, do it only once, front to back, the first day. Await messages from your shoulder joints the next day to see how much you can expect of yourself. If they ache, soak in a warm tub and keep them warm and relaxed until all the ache is gone. Use the ache as an indication that maybe you need a gentler exercise right now. You can come back to this when you're ready.

The muscle you're after here is called the "deltoid." It forms a kind of cap over the top of the shoulder joint, spreading out widely across the outer end of the collarbone, the top of the shoulder, and partly down in back across the wing bone or "scapula." From this wide beginning, it comes down to more or less a point to connect to the outside and almost the center of your arm bone. ("The cap his mother made him?")

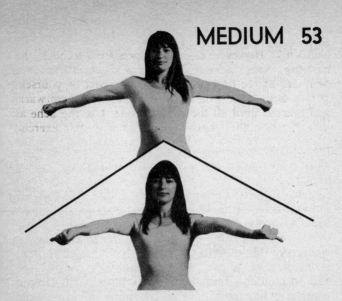

Stand with your feet apart for balance. ◇ Hold your arms straight out front at shoulder level, fists touching.

Turn your fists in so your thumbs are down and then turn them out so the insides of your fists are way up. ◇ Now add a bounce to the motion: Turn them up and over in a large half circle (as if you were drawing two half circles in opposite directions with your thumbs). ◇ At the same time start moving your arms slowly out to your sides, still with the bouncing half circles with your fists. ◇ Go back as far as you can; and then, still bouncing your fists in half circles, move your arms to the front again.

Be careful to get the motion mainly from the shoulder joint, not just in the lower arm! If anything hurts, if you get little sharp pains in your shoulder joints, if the joints begin to ache, *stop for the day!*

CAREFUL! VERY TOUGH ON OLD SHOULDER INJURIES!

The "deltoid" muscle being worked on here should really be divided into three parts—front, back, and center. The front portion helps the arm move forward, the back portion helps the arm move back, and the center portion moves the arm up away from the body. But they do *all work together to assist each other!* They work their hardest when the arm is at shoulder level or higher.

Cheat if it hurts! Lower your arms a little. The twisting motion included in the exercise is to get at the muscle from as many different directions as possible while at the same time using the joint as much as possible. Never do this exercise so much that you make your shoulder ache. If you can judge carefully, you will be able to continue developing slowly but steadily. If you make it ache, you'll have to take time off to recover. Take your time and you'll soon have very useful shoulders. These are the muscles that make you look broad-shouldered, so don't do more than you want.

KEEP AN EYE ON YOUR SHOULDERS. HOT SOAKS AND MASSAGE FOR THE OVERDOSE.

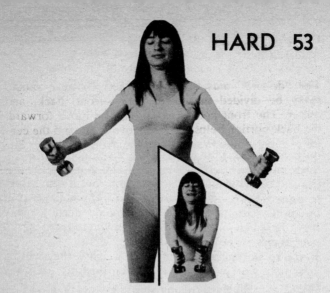

Stand with your feet apart for balance. ◊ Take some light weights in your hands. ◊ Hold your arms straight out front at shoulder level, fists touching.

Lift your arms up and over as you turn your thumbs under and then up and over as you turn the inside of your fist up. ◊ Make a tall half-oval shape with your thumbs, bounding up above shoulder level and down to shoulder level again. If it does not bother your shoulders at all, you can slowly increase the weight in your hands. ◊ Keeping up this twisting arm movement, start slowly moving your arms out to the sides, then as far back as possible, then forward again.

Make sure you get as much motion as possible in the shoulder joint itself. Turn your arm *in the socket each way as far as possible!* Don't start with heavy weights! Work up slowly!

DO EASIER VERSIONS FIRST!

Broad and beautiful shoulders! No effort (well, maybe some) at all. As you work your way up with the weights you will be making them not only broader but also much more useful. Men have a lot more muscle across the shoulders than women to begin with. With any steady weight work at all you can develop your shoulders to be almost as broad as you choose them to be. There's no need to be violent about it. If you are only consistent with the exercise it's going to happen. Such muscle not only looks good and is useful for lifting and carrying and many other jobs but it also serves to protect your shoulders from injury. If you have, built in, more strength than you commonly need for any task, there is no need to worry when you're faced with a new, tough, or heavy job to do.

If you're working with adjustable weights, they will be your only worry. Be sure to tighten them up each day before you begin.

Women who are serious mountain or rock climbers, trapeze artists, or swimmers may want to use the weights. Otherwise, you don't really need them unless you are *very* narrow-shouldered.

DO WORRY ABOUT ADJUSTABLE WEIGHTS! CHECK THEM EVERY DAY!

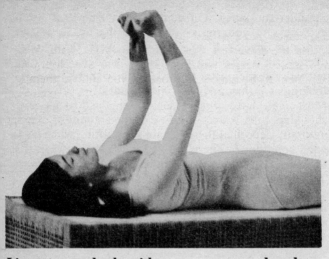

Lie on your back, either on a narrow bench or head down on a slant board.

(A board leaning against your bed is fine; just make sure it's firmly planted). If being head down makes you dizzy, use a straight bench (and don't hold your breath).

Have your elbows slightly bent! ◊ Fists up overhead so that you can see them.

With both arms, as if you were turning two steering wheels in opposite directions without your hands twisting, make small circles. ◊ Reverse directions on the imagined steering wheels. ◊ When you feel able—today, tomorrow, next week —start making the circles larger and larger. ◊ Be sure to work in both directions.

WATCH OUT FOR SHOULDER OR ELBOW CATCHES! IT'S BETTER TO DO FEW AND WAIT TO SEE WHAT TOMORROW BRINGS.

Lying down is the way to develop the chest muscles *without* developing the muscles across the top of the shoulder too much. Put your hands up on your shoulders next to your neck—these are the muscles which will also develop if you choose to work through this exercise in a standing position. That's great for men, but most women want to develop their chests without it looking as if they had been working at it.

Most men have much more strength through their shoulders than women because of the amount of muscle naturally deposited there. It looks beautiful (when it's in good condition). There are very few men so weak that they need this exercise. But if you are, don't worry There is no shame in using this exercise. But there is shame in just letting yourself go completely! If you don't want to build, but just tighten or tone, this is the exercise to stick with.

ie on your back, on a narrow bench or head down
n a slant board, if you're female. ◇ Stand if
ou're male, for this one. ◇ Have light weights in
our hands. ◇ Bend your elbows slightly, put
our hands out in front of your face.

lake small circles with both arms as if moving two
eering wheels in opposite directions without twist-
ig your hands. ◇ Reverse direction on the imag-
ied wheels. ◇ As you can, make the circles
irger and larger, then smaller and smaller. ◇
lake the weights heavier and heavier day by day.

ON'T INCREASE THE WEIGHTS TOO QUICK-
Y! DEVELOP SLOWLY!

lore than likely, most men would choose this exercise
r a *beginning*. It's a good one, getting at the arms,
ands, chest, and shoulders all at once.
tart with a light weight, whether you're male or female,
tanding or lying down, to increase the circulation a

little first. Work fast for a while with the lighter weigh and then move on to whatever weight you've built up t over a period of time.

If you're a female you may not want to carry the mus cle developing any further than this exercise will tak you. If so, do at least a few from a standing positio each time. Use some of your lighter weights, otherwis you'll have muscles that are too uneven, very wea ones next to quite strong ones.

All the shoulder muscles need to be strong enough t take care of each other. Men, you can go on to th tougher exercises if you want. Women, once you've go the muscles well developed, take up some occupatio that'll keep them in good condition. Make bread (n electric kneaders allowed). Give back rubs. Scru floors. Play tennis.

Women: Whether you're small or large in the breas over the chest muscle, you'll look better if the muscl is in good condition.

and with your feet planted well apart. ◇ Squat
floor to pick up weights.

---

o make it easier, pull weights in close to body before
ing. Work up to using reasonably heavy weights in
ch hand.

---

eeping your elbows slightly bent, put your hands
t in front of your face.

---

ake small circles into the center, up toward your
ad and around, for a while. ◇ Then make small
rcles into the center, down toward your waist,
d around. ◇ Make the circles smaller and
naller and larger and larger. ◇ Use heavier and
avier weights. ◇ Give your body something to
ink about: Use uneven weights in your hands for
while. ◇ Then lean over a little from the waist
r a while (forward or back).

Are you in a hurry for results? After you're in reason
able shape, do the exercise until tired, seven or eigh
times a day!!

DO THIS ONLY AFTER WORKING UP FROM
THE MEDIUM VERSION!

Don't do just exercises in which you're lifting weight
and developing muscles! Be good to your body. It i
not in good condition if you never do any long-distanc
walking or running—or if you never do any flexibilit
exercises! Especially if you're going to be lifting ver
heavy weights! And don't lift very heavy weights fo
your chest if you haven't yet strengthened your bacl
with weights.

If you ever decide you've had it with the big muscl
stuff do yourself a favor and descend slowly, over
period of a year or even two, from the heavy weight
down to the light ones. Taper off and prevent th
"sags." Taper off in the amount of food that you ea
also. That is one of the biggest problems with all ded
icated athletes. The muscle doesn't turn to fat! Bu
once they stop developing muscle, the food that onc
was turned into muscle now turns into fat. Protein o
not—if you don't need food, if you don't work, it'
going to turn into flab!

nd barefoot.

up a sturdy bar in a standard doorway just above
r head. Check it to be sure it's tight. Put a pillow
pillows) on the floor under the bar.

ce both hands firmly around the bar.

you terribly weak in lifting your arms? Reach the
ker hand up to the bar *with help* from the stronger
d first and then put the stronger hand up. You can
it!

your weight down gently, keeping your feet on
floor, but bending your knees. ◊ Try to twist
r body first a little to one side and then a little
the other. ◊ If your hands feel strong and se-
e, try to let your body weight hang from the
. ◊ Once you feel safe and sure with your body
ght hanging, bounce your knees a little to in-
ase the pull on your shoulders and hands. ◊

405

When you feel completely sure of yourself (take
as much time as you need, weeks even, don't take
chances!), take your feet off the floor for a few
seconds at a time.

If you are very weak, have someone else put your bar
up and tighten it!

THIS EXERCISE IS HARD ON STIFF SHOULDERS! CHOOSE SOMETHING EASIER FROM THE "GUIDE."

Everyone needs at least one bar to hang from somewhere in his home. If you don't have one you should
buy it or make it. It's the only thing you need that you
probably cannot make do without. Almost anything else
you can makeshift, but what would your doctor say if
you told him, "Well, doctor, it was this way. I fell off
the door frame." (And would I be embarrassed!)

Once you do have one and have it up, *be sure, every
day, that you check its tightness before hanging your
full body weight from it! In fact, check it each time you
use it and see to it that you train any kids around to do
the same thing!* My younger son used to swing out my
bedroom door (that's where I have my bar) every night
after bidding me "Good night." You can guess the
rest. One night he swung out . . . and out . . . and down
flat on his back! We tighten ours up, now, every time
we use it! If you're going to put a low one in for smaller
kids, put it in a closet door! Again, I can tell you from
experience, it's a real hazard anywhere else!

TIGHTEN THE BAR!

406

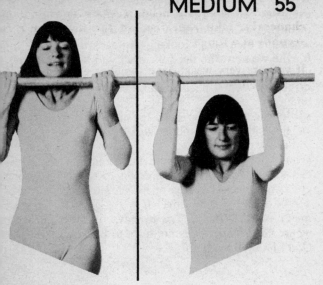

nd barefoot.

ve a sturdy bar in a doorway. Check its tightness.
ve a thick pad or rug underneath the bar.

ab hold of the bar securely with your hands. ◊
mp up so that your chin is level with the bar. ◊
t yourself slowly down until your feet touch the
or. ◊ Keep that up until you can let yourself
wn slowly every time.

may take weeks—be consistent!

w try to raise yourself a little more slowly—
thout the jump. Keep trying until you can do
t well. It will always feel like work. ◊ Now try
increase the number of times you can do it in a
w.

THE EASIER VERSION FIRST!

Again, you men are bound to outdo women in thes
exercises because of the natural gift of heavier muscl
through the shoulders. A few extra hours sneaked i
when the men aren't looking can even things up a littl
for the women who need the ability to hold your weigh
up for mountain climbing or such stuff. Men are heavie
in general. They need the extra muscle to move thei
bodies.

All of us *should* be able to support our own bod
weight with our shoulders and hands. Very few of u
can today.

What I want is an overhead ladder in my front hall.
can see me now, swinging down to the front door t
greet my guests. Houses really should be built to kee
people healthy and active, if we're going to spend s
much time in them. Try to have at least one roor
where your family does not have to be careful, or quier
Don't fix that room up!

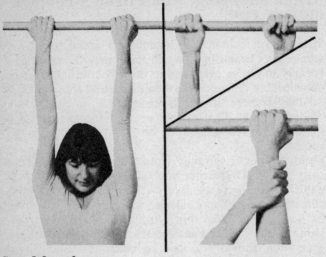

Stand barefoot.

Put a sturdy bar high up in a doorway. Check its tightness. Have a thick pad or rug underneath the bar.

Jump up to grab hold of the bar with your chin up close to it.

Let yourself down slowly until your feet are hanging just off the floor with your full weight on your straightened-out arms and shoulders. ◇ Bend your knees if you have to. ◇ Let your feet down, jump up again, and slowly lower yourself. ◇ After weeks of struggling and slowly gaining strength, raise yourself back up from the straightened arm position instead of jumping to get your chin back up to the bar.

Keep breathing! No grunting! No snorting! Just a slow steady struggle! Have you made it? Feel great? Try it one-handed.

DO THIS EXERCISE ONLY AFTER LOTS OF OTHER SHOULDER WORK OVER A LONG PERIOD OF TIME!

Straight-arm chinning is something I stand back and admire. It's beautiful to watch those muscles work. Especially if you've ever tried to do it yourself! It's really unbelievably difficult! But then look at all those beautiful lady trapeze artists, swinging away as though it's nothing at all! That is one of the (formerly secret) things I always wanted to be. Who knows? Maybe someday!

Children should certainly learn very early to hang by their hands. The earlier you let them do it, the more natural it is for them. Every school yard and, in cold climates, every school, inside, whether there is a gym or not, should have things for children to hang and swing from (by the hands!). We of the disadvantaged generation should try *now* to catch up. Bodies are rather wonderful! It's almost never too late!

Lie on your belly. ◇ Toes pointed. ◇ Put your hands on the floor, elbows bent, by your shoulders.

Push up with your hands and try to get your middle up off the floor.

If you can't, just keep trying every day until you can, or if you're very weak, go back to some of the other exercises in the "guide" that you find easier.

If you can, lift your belly right up off the floor and rest your weight on the tops of your feet (toes pointed) and your hands, and begin to walk along the floor with your hands, dragging your feet.

WEAK SHOULDERS? LOOK IN THE "GUIDE."

It's important to get your shoulder muscles strong and keep them strong, both in pushing and pulling directions. If you can't get your middle up off the floor, try to drag yourself along with your lower arms, using both to pull your body forward. Weak shoulders or injured ones will need easier, more basic exercises, but when you are ready to move on, this is a good beginner.

Don't let your arms remain weak while you work on your legs and your middle! *It is important that the muscles be able to depend on each other!* When you do finally manage to lift your body up and pull it along by using your hands, you'll feel your whole body working *with* your shoulders.

It's an exercise that feels good. Any little sharp pains in your shoulders *may* mean you've got small calcium deposits. In that case go back to flexibility exercises. Pushing your shoulders against those deposits will only make them *more* painful!

Get down on your hands and knees on the floor. ◊
Turn your toes under to help you get a grip on the
floor. ◊ Lean forward to get your back in a
straight line from your knees to your head.

Jump your arms apart, on the floor, and back together.

Keep your back in a straight line the whole time. Even
let your bottom sag *in* a little! *Don't let your bottom
stick up!*

EASY VERSION FIRST, PLEASE!

This is pretty hard, but it's also pretty good.
Make sure you have no discomfort at all with the easy
exercise before beginning this one. Putting pressure,
steady pressure, on a painful joint is bad enough. Putting bouncing pressure on it is just no good at all! You
can undo an awful lot of good in just a couple of
bounces. It's not worth it!

But for strengthening good shoulders, this exercise is great. It gets your chest muscles pretty well too. And your upper back. And your arms and hands. And even your back and belly. (And your toes?) Everything counts. You just might need strong and flexible toes someday—if for nothing else, to do this exercise and the next one.

You won't be able to do too many of these the first time.

WATCH OUT FOR YOUR SHOULDER JOINTS!

Lie on your belly on the floor. ◇ Turn your toes under. ◇ Put your hands on the floor, by your shoulders, elbows bent. ◇ Pick your middle up off the floor.

Keeping your body rigid, jump up off the floor with both your hands and your feet at the same time and, of course, come back down to the original position. ◇ If you become strong enough, try clapping your hands and feet together in midair.

Warm up first! Gently to begin with!

THIS ONE IS FOR SUPER ATHLETES ONLY!

I've never seen a girl who could do this exercise with the hands and feet clapping! Probably acrobatically trained women could; I'm sure there are others . . . I just haven't met them.

But I have met quite a few men who could! And *age does not seem to make the difference! Condition cer-*

tainly does! Several men in their seventies I know find it apparently quite easy (fifty years of practice makes a difference?) and some seventeen-year-olds fall flat on their faces!

Most kids are at a disadvantage. For average people, there is very little real physical work left to do in the world. Our bodies show the results. Unless you look for it, you could go your whole life without ever doing anything as tough as this type of push-up! Look for it! You'll look better for it! Don't be unhappy if you end up having to do hard physical labor. Be grateful!

ALWAYS WARM UP SLOWLY BEFORE ATTEMPTING THIS TYPE OF PUSH-UP!

Sit on the floor, with both legs folded to the floor, your feet to the left. ◊ Turn so your hands are leaning on the floor in front of your right thigh.

Bend your elbows to lower your chest to the floor, and then straighten them to rise back up. ◊ Keep your head up! Keep your back arched! ◊ Do the same movement on the other side.

NOT FOR BAD SHOULDERS OR ELBOWS! LOOK IN THE "GUIDE" FOR OTHER EXERCISES.

If you haven't sat on the floor for years and don't think you can make it—don't! Sit in a sturdy armchair instead. Also, if your arms are very weak, a chair can make it a little easier for you.

Sit a little to one side, put both hands on one arm of the chair, and, bending your elbows, lower your chest to the arm of the chair, keeping your head

417

up and back arched. ◇ **Then straighten your elbows to come back to the original position.** ◇ **Do an equal number of times on each side.**

If you are quite weak, do this exercise only one or two times on each side. If one side seems weaker than the other, start on the weak side and do the last one on the weak side, until finally, after a few weeks, they seem to be equally strong. This is a good rule to follow with all exercises. When the sides seem equal, continue day by day to build them up evenly.

This muscle at the back of the upper arm, being used here, is called the "triceps." "Tri" means three, and "ceps" means head. The word sounds weird, but it only means that there are three attachments at the upper end to give the muscle added strength.

Stand barefoot facing a wall. ◇ Keep your heels flat on the floor. ◇ Keep your hands on the wall. ◇ Back your feet away from the wall.

Bend your elbows to let your chest lean into the wall. ◇ Straighten your elbows to push yourself away from the wall. ◇ Keep your heels down! Keep your bottom sagging in! Keep your back arched! Keep your head up!

BAD SHOULDERS? TRY THE EXERCISE WITH YOUR FEET CLOSE TO THE WALL.

If your balance is good, you can begin the series with this exercise, from the standing position—but you must be sure your position is correct, not only because in doing a standard push-up your position must be very close to this, but also because this position gives you a great stretch for the backs of your legs!

Try hard to have your heels as far away from the wall as you possibly can but keeping them still down on the floor. Don't let your bottom stick up! Sag it in! It may be—it quite often is—easier to do the exercise the wrong way, and you may even come out of the session feeling virtuous. But in the long run you'll have to do it the right way in order to develop the right muscles.

As you exercise you will feel the backs of your legs easing up—they begin not to feel quite so stretched. Move your heels back just a little farther when this happens. Keep them feeling stretched!

It's a strange exercise for the backs of the upper arms, isn't it? My son has just rightly said, "You'd better tell how much that can make you ache" (not in the arms—in the backs of the legs)!

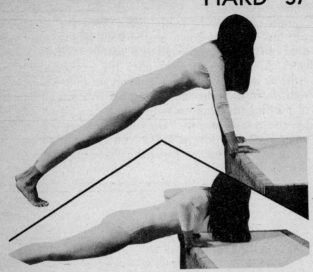

Stand facing a flight of stairs. ◊ **Lean over from your standing position to place your hands on the fourth step.** ◊ **Keep your body in a straight line from your feet to your shoulders.**

Bend your elbows to let your chest come down. ◊ **Push your elbows up straight to lift your chest.**

You are doing push-ups against the stairs.

Keep your body straight! And your bottom sagging in! ◊ **Then move down, when you can, to: the third step, and the second, and the first.**

Wow!

DO THIS ONE ONLY AFTER EASIER VERSIONS.

Now you're really getting down to work! Give yourself time—don't try to go too fast! Day after day do a slow, steady build-up until you can do as many as you'd like to be able to do.

I know one guy—he really doesn't look the type—who can and does get down on the floor and do two hundred push-ups as though it's nothing—*every day!* I can't do one *really* good one! It's embarrassing! All girls, as well as boys, should be taught to use their arms well, from the time they're infants. We are all capable of pushing up our own weight, given half a chance.

Dis-use is truly mis-use! Do you remember the old saying, "Use it or lose it"? But you really don't lose it! Your unused muscles just hang there making you feel mortified!

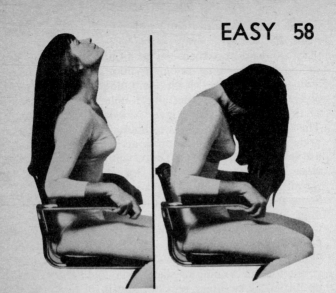

Sit in a chair. ◊ Hold on tightly to the arms. ◊ Or, better yet, sit cross-legged on the floor; keep your back up straight, hold your ankles, pull your shoulders down a little.

Let your head fall forward loosely, let your head fall back loosely.

DO THIS EXERCISE JUST ONCE, AND GENTLY, THE FIRST DAY! DON'T DO IT AT ALL IF YOU HAVE NECK PROBLEMS, WITHOUT YOUR DOCTOR'S OKAY!

If you have a stiff or painful neck it's no time to start doing anything violent. Even with this easy exercise, it would be a lot more comfortable if you started with a hot bath in which you can get way down to soak your neck for a while.

Remember, *heat loosens up the joints!* That means there will be a little more room between the bones, or vertebrae, that run down your back. Joints tend to be pulled together more tightly when they get cold, either from the weather, during sleep, when your body temperature drops, or when you sit around more than you should. *Movement of any kind will build up your body temperature.* Warm clothes will help you hold your body heat in close (especially double and triple layers of thin stuff or a single layer of pile fabric like fur). The idea of such clothes is to hold air still next to your body so that it can pick up your body heat and then use it to keep you warm. That's why you should really wear "the fur side inside," for the most possible warmth.

Some people very definitely throw out more body heat than others. For us colder people, a combination of warmer clothes and maybe a walk or a little running in place to pre-warm us helps a whole lot. But you're not likely to be doing a lot of walking if your neck brothers you, let alone running in place. You could try warmed-up turtleneck sweaters, plus hot towels for ten or fifteen minutes, before trying the exercise, instead of a bath.

Sit on a chair. ◇ Hold on tightly to the arms. ◇
Or, better yet, sit cross-legged on the floor. ◇
Keep your back up very straight. ◇ Hold on to
your ankles. ◇ Hunch your shoulders and then
pull them down. ◇ Put your chin on your chest.
◇ Jut your lower jaw forward to get your lower
teeth as far over your upper lip as possible and
keep it there.

Pull your neck up high and stretch your chin
way back. ◇ Then stretch the back of your neck
way up high and pull your chin forward to your
chest again.

You should feel the pull first down the front of your
neck and then down the back of your neck and into
your shoulders.

**DO THIS EXERCISE ONLY AFTER THE EASY
VERSION.**

Be sure, as usual, to begin with the basic relaxing exercise. You can find it in the "guide." If your neck is good and relaxed before you begin, you'll be less likely to get a stiff neck. With a combination of the basic relaxing exercise and a little warmth you can work quite a bit and never feel an ache. *Especially if you remember to use the relaxing exercise again, as the finishing touch to any series of neck exercises!*

This exercise is the one to do if you have a double chin. A double chin hangs down in the middle. Jowls hang down on the sides. If you have one you most likely have both, but you should know the difference anyway.

Remember that a lot of sagging muscles are not only from lack of use but also from lack of the right food. All of us need to eat lots of protein and move much more than we generally do. Eating protein and *not* moving more will not help because your body will only use what it needs—and only a working muscle has an appetite for protein. If you don't make a "move" to help it, your body will not make a muscle.

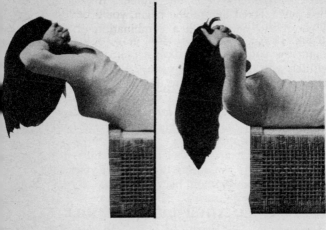

Lie across a bed, head and shoulders over the edge.
◇ Jut your lower jaw forward to get your lower
teeth as far over your upper lip as possible and
keep it there.

Face down first: Clasp your hands behind your
head and pull your head up against pressure from
your hands. ◇ Then clasp your hands in front of
your head and push your head down against pressure from your hands.

Face up next: Clasp your hands in front of your
forehead and pull your head up against pressure
from your hands. ◇ Clasp your hands in back of
your head and push your head down against pressure from your hands.

Not too many to begin with! Not too much pressure to
begin with! Be sure to keep breathing steadily!

The stronger your arms are the stronger your neck muscles can become. The stronger your arms are the more

you can make your neck muscles hurt. Your body learns day by day, little by little. With practice and a little more effort each day, you can learn almost anything. With time you can have your neck wonderfully strong. If you try to get it that way by the day after tomorrow you may only have a pain in the neck that will last you the rest of your life. Take your time! Build up the pressure day by day. Do it every single day or even twice or three times a day if you want to move faster—*and still, no matter how strong you become, remember to do the basic relaxing exercise before and after every session!*

This is a good exercise. You get your hands, arms, and shoulders at the same time that you get your neck . . . *and* your abdominals and back!

NEVER HOLD YOUR BREATH WHILE EXERCISING!

Sit on the floor.

If you really can't do that, use a chair, but floor sitting is preferred.

If you're sitting in a chair, hold on to the arms and be sure to keep hold! ◊ If you can, sit on the floor, knees out, ankles crossed, hands holding on to ankles, shoulders pulled gently down. ◊ Let your head fall gently forward.

Roll your head, loosely and gently, completely around in a circle, first in one direction, then in the other.

If it makes you dizzy, just do it once the first day. If you do get dizzy, stay on the floor until the dizziness passes, or if you're in a chair, hold on to the arms until you're sure you're all right again. Dizziness does not mean that you shouldn't do it again! It only means that you haven't been doing it! Try it again just once a day, tomorrow and the next day and the next . . . the dizziness will most likely go. Keep trying!

If it hurts anywhere—read on. If your neck really is very stiff and painful, a warm woolen scarf worn night and day for a while should help . . . or try a turtleneck sweater.

If you're in really poor condition you may find that even this exercise will make your neck stiff. So be sure to start with only one circle in each direction the first day. *All* the way around!

This simple and relaxing exercise should *always* begin and end each of the following versions. If you ever forget it, you'll be surprised how stiff in the neck you can get! These later versions are much harder on your neck than they feel while you're doing them.

The neck is a difficult area to live with once it becomes stiff. From that moment on your whole body has to do the job your neck did for itself before. If you have ever had a stiff or painful neck, you know the misery and discomfort of having actually to turn your whole body to look at something that is just a little to one side . . . or the slow dismal dance at street corners just to see if a car is coming. It was during my "bad neck period" that I developed one of my first opinions. I firmly believe that pedestrian crossings should be in the center of the block and not at the corners. That way you can only get run down from two directions instead of many. If you do have a painful neck be sure to cross, if you can, only where there are lights. You can't afford to jog! It hurts!

If you're trying to get over motion sickness of any kind, start the first day slowly and work over a period of days rolling your head faster and faster. Quit when you get dizzy!

Sit on the floor.

If you can't sit on the floor for some reason, this exercise can be done in a chair. Hold on if you need to.

If you can: Sit on the floor, knees out, ankles crossed, hands holding on to ankles, shoulders pulled down (shrug them up and then pull them down as far as possible), back up very straight. ◇ Stretch your neck as far forward as you can.

Roll it completely around in a circle, twice in one direction and then twice in the other. ◇ Keep your back straight, your shoulders down, your neck stretched.

DON'T DO THIS ONE IF YOU STILL GET DIZZY ON THE EASY VERSION, OR IF IT HURTS ANYWHERE.

You should not continue to do the neck relaxing or stretching exercises once you become dizzy. Stop, and wait for the next day or, if you are really anxious to improve, try it again later the same day.

The neck, or cervical area of the spine, has more freedom of movement than any other part of the spine. Most of the movement comes from just the first two vertebrae (or bones of the spine), and the whole spinal column, arranged like thirty-three building blocks, with one vertebra piled on top of the other, is held together by the most fantastically closely knit ligaments. Ligaments are a kind of connective tissue but have more elastic tissue than other types of connective tissue. Besides having this tissue to hold the vertebrae together, the spinal column has cushions between the vertebrae to hold them apart.

The ligaments sometimes, with lack of use, can really lose their elasticity. The muscles in the neck area also can become stiff from lack of use. You can almost always regain flexibility with constant practice and use. You have everything to gain and nothing to lose (except a stiff neck).

Sit on the floor.

Floor sitting is preferred for this exercise, but it's possible to do it from a chair. Be sure to sit well back in the chair! Be very careful to work through the easy and medium versions first.

If you are able: Sit on the floor, knees out, ankles crossed.

Clasp your hands behind your head and pull gently with your hands as you press your head completely around in a circle, a couple of times in one direction and then a couple of times in the other direction. ◇ Then clasp your hands in front of your forehead and push gently with your hands as you press your head again completely around in a circle in one direction a couple of times, and then a couple of times in the other direction. ◇ After the first few times start increasing the pressure

from your hands, or try increasing the number of times you circle in each direction.

ONLY AFTER WORKING UP THROUGH EASIER VERSIONS FOR WEEKS!

Unless you're a wrestler or a boxer this one is going to be tough on you. It's easy enough to do, but not so easy to live through the consequences unless you begin the exercise in a rather gentle manner and work your way up. Why not try it the first day with just the barest of pressure from your hands and wait to see the next day just how your neck is taking to it? You can always do it harder the second day if you feel no results. Not too much harder! Build the pressure up very slowly over days!

The best way to recover if you've carried it too far is to get into a tub of hot water and scrunch down until your neck is covered by the water. If even the back of your head hurts put one or two folded washcloths behind your head on the tub. While the tub is running, throw a couple of towels over a radiator or any other hot spot. When you get out of the tub wrap one of these warm towels around your neck. When it cools, put that one on the radiator and use the other one. You can keep this towel switching up as long as you need to or want to.

If you do the exercise in a reasonable manner you should be able to increase the pressure from your hands day by day over a very long period of time. If you ever quit for a while be sure to start *without* full pressure on your neck.

Sit on the floor. ◊ Ankles crossed, your hands holding on to your ankles, and your back straight. ◊ Lean back a little and let your head hang back. ◊ Let your head and neck relax.

Roll them gently from one side to the other, keeping them back and rolling your cheeks as close to your shoulders as possible. ◊ Keep your shoulders down!

Are you new at this? Sit in an armchair if you can't get on the floor, and *stop immediately if you get dizzy!* Do just a few the first day and then relax! If you feel any aches after the first day, you should do only a few the first week and build very gradually. *These can really make you ache!* Be sure to stop after only one the first day!

NOT FOR UNCOMFORTABLE OR PAINFUL NECK PROBLEMS WITHOUT YOUR DOCTOR'S PERMISSION.

Few people today use their necks to the extent that our ancestors did thousands of years ago when they were both hunters and the hunted. Just imagine if you had to hunt for your food and be on the alert for danger at the same time! It's not like going to the supermarket! Your eyes, ears, and nose would be completely turned on *as your head and neck turned constantly* to scan for objects to attack or flee from. If a caveman ever stopped being alert, he didn't live long enough to develop jowls! Try this: Close your eyes and let your head roll slowly around. If you hear crickles, or if you get dizzy, *you* would have been a "dead caveman"!

About the only people today with full use of their necks are those in competitive sports!

If your neck gets stiff from this exercise the first day or two, wrap a warm towel around your neck. *Preferably wet!* Cover it with plastic wrap to keep it warm longer. There are the old built-in reflexes again—*"Fight* or *flight"*—working to keep us alive! *Our ancestors had to be in better shape than we are!*

ANY NECK PROBLEMS? ASK YOUR DOCTOR'S PERMISSION TO DO THIS EXERCISE.

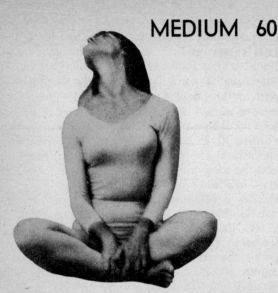

Sit in an armchair, or, better yet, sit on the floor, ankles crossed, knees out, hands grasping ankles. ◊ Pull your shoulders gently down. ◊ Keep your back straight.

Stretch your neck gently from side to side at the same time that you stretch it up. ◊ Turn your head to bring your nose directly over one shoulder. ◊ Then drop the top of your head back, tilting your chin up. ◊ From this position, stretch your chin up a little farther (you should feel the stretch). ◊ Always do the same movement to the other side too! ◊ Repeat—changing the stretching to a gentle bounce. ◊ Harder yet? Repeat—but add a chewing motion, jutting your chin way forward as you chew instead of bounce.

These neck movements are harder on you than they seem! Start with only one to each side, no matter how good your condition!

ARTHRITIC AND CERVICAL DISC PATIENTS, ANYONE WITH NECK PROBLEMS—ASK YOUR DOCTOR!

The neck seems to get stiffer, faster, than any other part of the body! *That was a warning!* Please believe me and *always do the easy variation* of this exercise *before* you begin this exercise—and *again after* you have finished it! *Every time!* If you get carried away with enthusiasm, try hot towels, hot tubs, turtleneck sweaters, and the easy variation of this exercise to ease the misery—*and don't push so hard next time!*

Besides developing neck flexibility, you are getting the muscle that, without proper attention, will give you jowls. Strangely enough, it is a facial muscle, but it seems to run down the neck to a point a little way under the collarbone! It starts at the corner of the mouth and gets wider as it travels down, a little like water if you let it run out the corners of your mouth with your chin tipped up! Just imagine it! It's messy, believe me!

CAUTION: IF YOU HAVE CERVICAL ARTHRITIS, PINCHED NERVES THAT GIVE YOU DISCOMFORT, OR PROBLEMS FROM WHIPLASH ACCIDENTS OR BREAKS, DO NOT DO THIS EXERCISE WITHOUT THE CONSENT OF YOUR DOCTOR!

Lie on your back across a bed or a bench. ◇ Hang your head and neck completely over the edge. ◇ Turn your head as far as possible to one side, tilting your chin slightly up toward the ceiling and jutting it forward.

Lift your head and turn it until your chin touches the opposite shoulder. ◇ Now turn your head and lower it to the original position. ◇ Do the exercise also to the opposite side.

NECK PROBLEMS? DON'T DO THIS ONE!

By hanging your head over the edge of the bed, you are increasing the amount of work your neck muscles have to do by making them lift your head up! You'll really feel the pull the first time from this position!
As you let your head drop back down, its weight will pull on the neck muscles, giving them a good stretch. This exercise gives you the most results for the time spent, *but*, again, do not do it without doing the easier version,

both before you start this one and after you have done as many of it as you want!

The neck is an almost unbelievable balancing system. It always makes me think of trying to juggle a basketball on top of a "five and dime" segmented snake, but you should see the muscles! Up and down and criss-crossing diagonally! It's a natural engineering job to give the most possible movement with the most possible strength! I can't bring myself to say "It's your neck"! But again, be careful!